Macroeconomy of Internet Sphere with Complex Numbers

Macroeconomy of Internet Sphere with Complex Numbers

Sergey Sergeevich Khrystenko

Writers Club Press
New York Lincoln Shanghai

Macroeconomy of Internet Sphere with Complex Numbers

Writers Club Press
an imprint of iUniverse, Inc.

For information address:
iUniverse
2021 Pine Lake Road, Suite 100
Lincoln, NE 68512
www.iuniverse.com

ISBN: 0-595-26322-4

Printed in the United States of America

INTRODUCTION

In the economy of the Internet sphere there is quite number of problems that need to be solved. Judge for yourselves:
- until recently, the Internet sphere has never been examined as an economic system;
- peculiarities of the Internet components haven't been worked out;
- peculiarities of the economic relations in the Internet sphere haven't been defined;
- essence of the categories—Internet value, Internet services, complex Internet product—hasn't been established;
- economic estimations of the Internet values are defined separately from the economic estimations of the Internet services;
- «On Line Time» (OLT) is not considered as an economic resource;
- the OLT resource is not included in the cost of the Internet services;
- specific features of the economic estimations connected with the movement of the Internet values and Internet services.

The economic criteria of the effectiveness of the use of resources in the framework of production, distribution, exchange and consumption have not been explained.

The outlines of these problems become clearer and significantly better understood if Internet values, Internet services and the OLT are examined in a three-dimensional space.

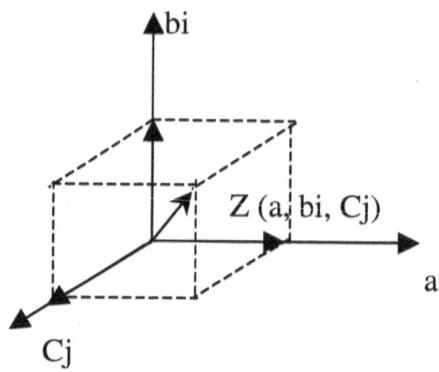

where (a) is the cost estimation of Internet values (computers, programmes etc.)

(bi) represents the expenses connected with the creation of
Internet services (OLT not included)

(Cj) is the cost estimation of the assimilated OLT resource.

The total Vector Z is formulated as follows: $Z = a + bi + Cj$

The Z vector assumes different values depending on the three components a, b and c.

If the particular OLT resource is not taken into account, the Z vector
is being examined in two-dimensional space, without the Cj
component.

If we look at the reproduction of the Internet sphere from this position,
i.e. without the «On Line Time» (OLT) resource, it will mean that
one of the basic Internet incoming resources is excluded. As a
result, the economic estimations are decreased by the amount of
not included OLT resource.

In the diagrams of the reproduction of the Internet sphere the following takes place:
- <u>equalities between separate parts</u> of the Internet values and Internet services (in the multibillion calculation) without taking into account the OLT resource become inequalities.
- <u>inequalities,</u> compiled without taking into account the OLT resource, become equalities for the same reason.

How is it possible to examine the process of the exchange of Internet values and Internet services on a macroeconomic level without taking into account the OLT resource, when the annual multibillion volume of the Internet values and Internet services is exchanged with another multibillion volume of values and services?

The exchange process may be explained only with real economic estimations, which include the OLT resource. Then you can see relationship existing between the internal parts of the Internet products in the annual reproduction process.

Some Internet researchers propose to examine the function of «demand and supply». This approach is taken from the theory of material production.

The deficiency of this approach is that it examines two types of relations: «production» and «consumption». In other words, in theory, a specific «surgical operation» is performed to remove two economic relationships: «distribution» and «exchange» in the Internet sphere.

In the square outlined by dashes I have shown the part of the relationship that is cut out.

Production	Distribution	Exchange	Consumption
A. «Production» process of Internet values ↓	«Distribution» process of Internet values ↓	«Exchange» process of Internet values ↓	«Consumption» process of Internet values ↓
B. «Production» process of Internet services ↓	«Distribution» process of Internet services ↓	«Exchange» process of Internet services ↓	«Consumption» process of Internet services ↓
C. «Production» process of complex Internet product	«Distribution» process of complex Internet product	«Exchange» process of complex Internet product	«Consumption» process of complex Internet product

After the above «surgical operation» only two types of relationships will remain:

Production	Consumption
A. «Production» process of Internet values ↓	«Consumption» process of Internet values ↓
B. «Production» process of Internet services ↓	«Consumption» process of Internet services ↓
C. «Production» process of complex Internet product	«Consumption» process of complex Internet product

Can we understand the economic issues of the Internet sphere if we
only examine the production and consumption of Internet values
and Internet services?

If we examine the economic relationships of the Internet in its curtailed
form then the following processes will remain unconsidered:

Distribution	*Exchange*
A. «Distribution» process of Internet values ↓	→ «Exchange» process of Internet values ↓
B. «Distribution» process of Internet services ↓	→ «Exchange» process of Internet services ↓
C. «Distribution» process of complex Internet product	→ «Exchange» process of complex Internet product

Without taking into consideration the relationship of «distribution»
and «exchange» it is impossible to understand the whole process
of movement of Internet values and Internet services.

Definitely, research cannot be confined to the framework of the two
relationships. This is not sufficient for the understanding of the
economic processes that take place on the Internet sphere. This is
a gross logical mistake.

The economic relationships of the Internet are interconnected. Each one of the economic relationships forms part of the common reproduction process and has its own specific characteristics:
- characteristics of the production of Internet values and Internet services;
- characteristics of the distribution of Internet values and Internet services;
- characteristics of the exchange of Internet values and Internet services;
- characteristics of the consumption of Internet values and Internet services.

When studying economic relationships we must:
- reject the old, petty dogmas of theory, which prevent us from moving forward;
- choose logical methods, which will be used in Internet theory;
- select numbers are going to use when calculating the expenditures and results of the Internet sphere;
- we should not compile a theory of the Internet sphere, by using only one or two economic relationships.

EPIGRAPH

Harmony of economic relations in the Internet sphere should be checked by algebra with complex numbers—quaternions.

CONTENTS

CHAPTER 1. COMPLEX APPROACH TO RESEARCH OF ECONOMIC PROCESSES

1. LOGIC APPROACH TO RESEARCH OF SOCIAL PRODUCTION

2. «NUMBER» AS INSTRUMENT OF RESEARCH FOR ECONOMIC PROCESSES

3. DEFINITION OF THE COMPLEX NUMBER

4. OPERATIONS ON COMPLEX NUMBERS IN ALGEBRAIC FORM

1. COMPLEX APPROACH TO RESEARCH OF ECONOMIC PROCESSES

If to assume that economic processes and economic relations are complex; economic interests are complex; social relations are complex then in the research of complex economic and social processes it is necessary to use a complex approach, together with complex knowledge, complex instruments and complex numbers. This is proven.[1]

In this logical sequence everything corresponds with each other. There are no defects. Everything is the way it should be.

We should not try to attempt avoiding the complex line. We should follow it everywhere. If we do not do it, the approach will be different from the complex one; it will not be complex.

The essence of the complex approach, from my point of view, is in application of the following:

1. Logic—dialectical method with categories: thesis, antithesis, synthesis;
   - inductive method;
   - deductive method etc.

2. Logical operations—operative system of formal logic;
3. Numbers—as an instrument of representing economic (social) processes;
4. Operations with numbers (technology of using numbers).

---

[1] The economic processes (social process) represent:

Thesis	Positive tendency in the process
Antithesis	Negative tendency in the process
Synthesis	Process in its entity (interactive process of positive and negative tendencies)

Depending on the kind of numbers used in economic processes, a complex approach can be modified in several different ways.

PECULIARITIES OF COMPLEX APPROACH TO RESEARCH OF ECONOMIC PROCESSES (WITH THE USE OF NATURAL NUMBERS)

1. Logic—dialectical method with categories: thesis, antithesis, synthesis;
   - inductive method;
   - deductive method etc.

2. Logical operations—operative system of formal logic;
3. Natural numbers—as an instrument, (mirror) representing economic processes
4. Operations with natural numbers (technology № 1).

PECULIARITIES OF COMPLEX APPROACH TO RESEARCH OF ECONOMIC PROCESSES (WITH THE USE OF REAL NUMBERS)

1. Logic—dialectical method with categories: thesis, antithesis, synthesis;
   - inductive method;
   - deductive method etc.

2. Logical operations—operative system of formal logic;
3. Real numbers—as an instrument, (mirror) reflecting economic processes
4. Operations using real numbers (technology № 2).

PECULIARITIES OF COMPLEX APPROACH
TO RESEARCH OF ECONOMIC PROCESSES
(WITH THE USE OF IRRATIONAL NUMBERS)

1. Logic—dialectical method with categories: thesis, antithesis, synthesis;
   - inductive method;
   - deductive method etc.

2. Logical operations—operative system of formal logic;
3. Irrational numbers—as an instrument (mirror) reflecting economic processes
4. Operations with irrational numbers (technology № 3).

PECULIARITIES OF COMPLEX APPROACH
TO RESEARCH OF ECONOMIC PROCESSES
(WITH THE USE OF COMPLEX NUMBERS)

1. Logic—dialectical method with categories: thesis, antithesis, synthesis;
   - inductive method;
   - deductive method etc.

2. Logical operations—operative system of formal logic;
3. Complex numbers—as an instrument (mirror) reflecting economic processes
4. Operations with complex numbers (technology № 4).

Research of economic processes, which take place in the Internet
sphere, requires not only knowledge but also an ability to use a
certain «surgical instrument» in the capacity of which numbers
are represented. Mathematical calculations occur in the quality of
technology related to the usage of the numbers.

Doing my research of the Internet economic processes, I concentrated
on three variants:

Variant I
- dialectic method
- logical operations
- real numbers
- mathematical operations using real numbers[2]

Variant II
- dialectic method
- logical operations
- complex numbers
- mathematical operations with complex numbers

Variant III
- dialectic method
- logical operations
- quaternions
- mathematical operations with numbers—quaternions

In the first variant simple mathematical operations are used. In the second variant the operations are a bit more complex. In the third
variant the operations are very complex.

The results achieved using these three variants differ one from the
other.

Every system of calculation has its virtues and vices.

---

[2] This variant has been analyzed in the book «Economy of Internet Sphere»

2. «NUMBER» AS INSTRUMENT OF RESEARCH OF ECONOMIC PROCESSES

In the hall of mirrors which we all visited one time or the other in our childhood, the mirrors' surfaces were distorted: some of them were convex, others concave. That affected our reflection in the mirror. These various transformations entertained us. Of course, it was funny.

I have mentioned the hall of mirrors in connection with different numbers the fact that a researcher of the economic processes who uses in his research—natural, irrational, real, imaginary, compound and super-compound (quaternions)—finds himself in an analogous situation. The numbers can be treated as a specific mirror that reflects economic processes.

Numbers, numbers, numbers—they are present everywhere, both in traditional and untraditional economy.

We don't ponder on the kind of numbers we use in economic calculations, although a lot depends on them. Real numbers reflect one depth of the economic processes; imaginary numbers show the other.

We should not be afraid of using untraditional numbers. If we look realistically, we can see that social sciences meet with exact sciences and they «go together»—next to real numbers, imaginary numbers and complex numbers quaternions.

Researching economic processes, we should not be afraid of fresh ideas and new horizons. Both in the area of the traditional and—even more importantly—untraditional economy, we should not find ourselves in the zone of old approaches, old opinions, thoughts and definitions.

It has taken thousands of years to define numbers. The numbers' theory has been widening and developing. For example, the ancient Greek mathematicians thought that only natural numbers were real.

In the times of Pythagoras a discovery was made in the area of numbers. Its essence consisted in the fact that there were not enough natural numbers, if one tried to put into practice the arithmetic calculations connected with the diagonal of a square (see Pythagorean Theory). There, the necessity of using real numbers came up.

I am not going to go deeper into the theory of the development of numbers' definition. It is enough if I say that <u>in our daily life we use real numbers and basic arithmetic calculations such as addition, subtraction, multiplication and division</u>. Only in some exceptional situation, do we raise a number to the nth power or extract the square root. In other words, <u>we use one type of numbers (real) and primitive mathematical apparatus (in our daily life).</u>

If we raise (A + B) to the third, fourth power, some very complex problems arise. Their essence consists in the fact that there are not enough real numbers (the ones that we use in our daily life) to solve the equations. Part of the equations can be solved only with the utilisation of <u>complex numbers</u>.

This situation partly explains the necessity of using new numbers and new methods of technology in calculations. There, everything looks the same as in daily life: some things can be measured by a simple ruler, some only using a logarithmic ruler. This is clear for everybody.

Because of this, mathematicians give the following example. <u>The system of the simple equations does not have a solution in the framework of real numbers,</u>

$$\begin{cases} X + Y = 10 \\ X \cdot Y = 40 \end{cases}$$

This system of equations looks simple. But the solutions for these equations lie beyond the borders of real numbers. Beyond the border of existing, traditional definitions, opinions and axioms. If we cross the line of «impossibility» imposed on us by real numbers, we will find solutions, but the journey towards these solutions leads through an arithmetically impossible operation—extracting the square root of negative number. The solution of the equation is as follows:

$$X = 5 \pm \sqrt{-15}; \quad Y = 5 \pm \sqrt{-15}$$

3. DEFINITION OF THE COMPLEX NUMBERS

In 1545 Italian mathematician G. Cardano made the first steps towards development of a theory of complex numbers.

In 1572 R. Bombelli established rules of an arithmetic operation on numbers.

In 1637 R. Decart offered a name for new numbers—«imaginary numbers».

In 1831 K.Gauss introduced a concept of an imaginary unity.

In the list of those who worked out complex numbers there are many well-known names—G. LaGrange, P.Laplas, Y.Bernulli, K.Vessel, G.Argan, and W.Hamilton.

The scope of usage of complex numbers is expanding with every passing year.

Complex numbers have incorporated the logic of the dialectical method.

Dialectic logic of construction of complex numbers.

Thesis	Real numbers—«a»
Antithesis	Imaginary number—«bi»
Synthesis	Complex number—Z = «a + bi»

The principal feature, being at the same time its advantage, of the «complex number» (complexus) is that with the help of complex numbers it is possible to reveal combination of several concepts, phenomena and processes as a whole. That is, the complex number <u>reveals the idea of compositions of concepts, compositions of processes and compositions of phenomena.</u>

Definition 1. Numbers—$a + bi$, where a and b—are real numbers, i—an imaginary unit—we will call them complex numbers.

Number a we will call a real part of a complex number, bi—an imaginary part of a complex number, b—a factor at an imaginary part. There are cases when it is possible that real numbers are equal to zero. If $a = 0$, a complex number bi refers to only imaginary. If $b = 0$, a complex number a + bi is equal to a and refers to only real. If $a = 0$ and $b = 0$ simultaneously, a complex number $a + bi$ is equal to zero. So, we have got that real numbers and only imaginary numbers are special cases of a complex number.

Record of a complex number as $a + bi$ is called an algebraic form of a complex number.

A complex number is represented either as a point with coordinates (a, b) or as a vector beginning in the center of coordinates (0,0) and ending in the point with coordinates (a, b) (see fig. 1).

Axis X is called a real axis, axis Y—an imaginary axis and a plane Z itself—a plane of complex numbers or Z-plane. Real numbers can be represented by points of a direct line as it is shown in figure 1.

Segments OA OB, can also represent these numbers, taking into account not only their length but the direction as well.

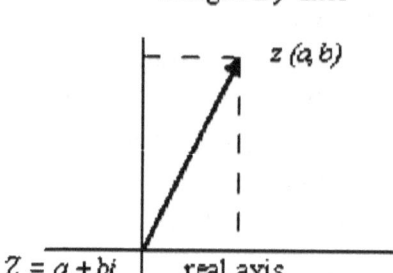

Two complex numbers $a + bi$ and $c + di$ are considered equal in only case when separately their real parts and factors at imaginary unit one are equal, that is $a + bi = c + di$, if $a = c$ and $b = d$.

4. OPERATIONS ON COMPLEX NUMBERS IN ALGEBRAIC FORM

Addition, subtraction, multiplication of complex numbers in algebraic form are carried out according to the rules of corresponding operations on multinomial.

a) $z_1 + z_2 = (a_1 + b_1i) + (a_2 + b_2i) = (a_1 + a_2) + (b_1i + b_2i)$

b) $z_1 - z_2 = (a_1 + b_1i) - (a_2 + b_2i) = (a_1 - a_2) + (b_1i - b_2i)$

c) $z_1z_2 = (a_1 + b_1i) \times (a_2 + b_2i) = a_1a_2 + a_1b_2i + a_2b_1i + b_1b_2i^2 = a_1a_2 + a_1b_2i + a_2b_1i - b_1b_2 = (a_1a_2 - b_1b_2) + (a_1b_2 + a_2b_1)i$

d)

$$\frac{z_1}{z_2} = \frac{a_1a_2 + b_1b_2}{a_2^2 + b_2^2} + \frac{(a_2b_1 - a_1b_2)i}{a_2^2 + b_2^2}$$

CHAPTER 2. CORRELATION OF FACTORS IN THE INTERNET SPHERE

1. «REAL» AND «IMAGINARY» PRODUCTIVE FORCES OF THE INTERNET SPHERE

2. «REAL» AND «IMAGINARY» ECONOMIC RELATIONS IN THE INTERNET SPHERE

3. COMPLEX CORRELATION OF FACTORS IN THE INTERNET SPHERE

1. «REAL» AND «IMAGINARY» PRODUCTIVE FORCES OF THE INTERNET SPHERE

There are many points of view regarding what a productive force of society is. In this work I will not classify positive and negative criteria in categories that are used in determining which economic processes are socially productive or useful and which are not.

In my opinion any socially organized process is productive provided that:
 – this kind of social activity is aimed at improving the welfare of the population of the country, and increasing the level of development of material, spiritual and transportation components, raising quality of health (life expectancy) etc.

If this kind of socially organized activity is aimed at decreasing the material, spiritual and transportation components as well as impairing the welfare of the population, then this process cannot be socially productive or beneficial.

These are principal criteria, which should be applied in the classification of labor in any country.

Generally, the productive force of society can be shown as follows:

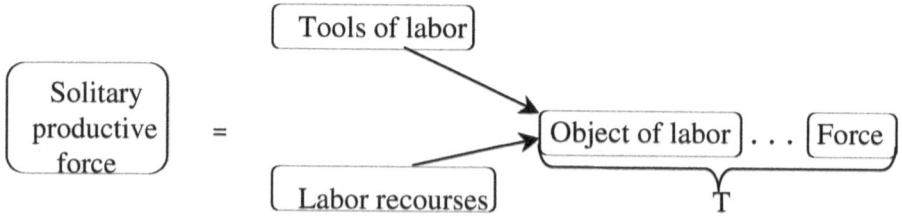

Where, «tools» take part in the process of making material values (or services);

«Labor recourses», is the live force, which puts in motion all the factors of the process of making material values (or services);

«Object of labor» is the object upon which tools and labor recourses are applied.

As a result of system correlation of these three factors of production either material of non-material service are created.

System correlation of mentioned factors is possible if they are united by economic relations.

I consider Internet sphere as an economic system that consists of two kinds of productive forces:

A) Productive forces oriented for creation of Internet values:

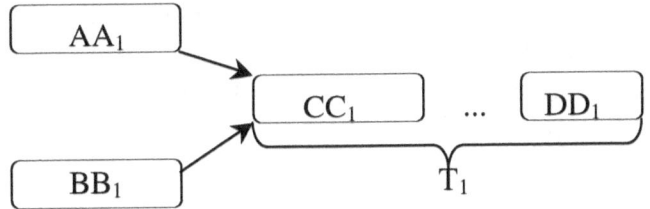

where AA_1—instruments of labor of first kind of productive forces of Internet sphere;

BB_1—labor resources of first kind of productive forces of Internet sphere;

CC_1—object of labor of first kind of productive forces of Internet sphere;

DD_1—product of labor of first kind of productive forces of Internet sphere;

T_1—interaction time of factors of first kind of productive forces of Internet sphere.

B) Productive forces of second kind oriented for creation of Internet services:

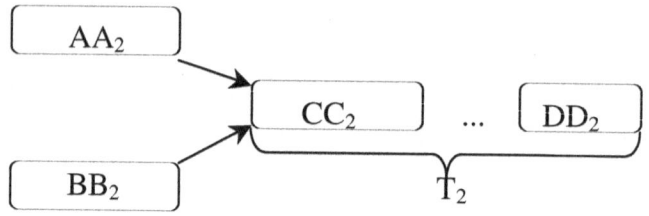

Where AA_2—instruments of labor of second kind of productive forces of Internet sphere;

BB_2—labor resources of second kind of productive forces of Internet sphere;

CC_2—object of labor of second kind of productive forces of Internet sphere;

DD_2—product of labor of second kind of productive forces of Internet sphere;

T_2—interaction time of factors of second kind of productive forces of Internet sphere.

C) Complex productive forces of Internet sphere:

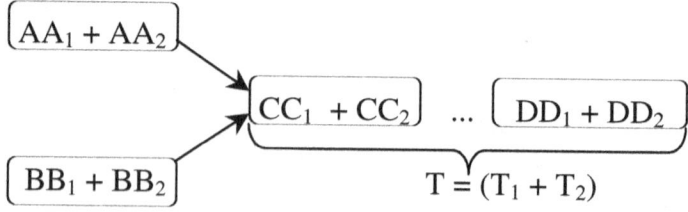

Where $AA_1 + AA_2$—complex instruments of labor of first and second
        kind of productive forces of Internet sphere;

$BB_1 + BB_2$—complex labor resources of first and second kind of
        productive forces of Internet sphere;

$CC_1 + CC_2$—complex object of labor of first and second kind of
        productive forces of Internet sphere;

$DD_1 + DD_2$—complex product of labor of first and second kind
        of productive forces of Internet sphere;

$T = (T_1 + T_2)$—complex interaction time of factors of first and
        second kind of productive forces of Internet sphere.

System interaction of factors of Internet sphere is possible, if they are
        united by economic relations.

Thus, if we look at Internet sphere with both eyes through «material»
        and «non-material» criteria using complex numbers we shall get
        the formula:

Thesis: Real numbers—«a»
Antithesis: Imaginary numbers—«bi»
Synthesis: Complex numbers—$Z = a + bi$

Thesis   Real productive forces of Internet sphere
        - production of Internet values

Antithesis   Imaginary productive forces of Internet sphere
        - production of Internet services

Synthesis   Complex productive forces of Internet sphere
        - production of Internet values and services

We classified productive forces of Internet sphere using terminology of
        complex numbers theory for material and non-material criteria.
        This is from the one point of view. From the other one we made a
        classification using real, imaginary and complex numbers.

We considered separately the productive forces and economic relations. This kind of autonomous consideration must be supplemented by a complex approach. The idea is that productive forces cannot function outside economic relations. Only within the frames of such the functioning of productive forces is possible. Otherwise, what kind of connection can exist between factors of production: tools, labor recourses and objects of labor?

2. «REAL» AND «IMAGINARY» ECONOMIC RELATIONS IN INTERNET SPHERE (CLASSIFICATION OF ECONOMIC RELATIONS)

The people, who once have come in touch with the Internet sphere ask themselves:

What kind of economic relations exist in the Internet sphere?

What is the structure of economic relations in the Internet sphere?

What are specifications of economic relations in the Internet sphere?

Do economic relations manifest themselves in «pure» form or are they complex?

Perhaps, some economic relations of the Internet sphere act as «real economic relations» and some as «imaginary economic relations»?

There are many questions.

To understand economic relations in the Internet sphere we should not draw a rough parallel with those been, which have formed in the timber or chemical industries.

The Internet sphere is not a traditional sphere and should be viewed differently; with a special attitude.

If you take part in making computers or software or if you have bought a computer, or software, you have logged in to Internet, in all these cases you become a participant in the economic relations taking place in this sphere of social production.

Economic relations, which have been formed in the Internet sphere, are the connecting link, which exists between all the parts taking part in this system.

When entering economic relations people do not ask themselves about the kind and peculiarity of these relations. For some people these questions do not have any importance while for others, e.g. for economists and lawyers they arise and require a response.

In fact, if we divide all values into two groups: material and non-material then we can do the same with the whole system of economic relations—we can divide it into two large components:

Thesis   Economic relations in the material values sphere of economics we shall indicate them as—«a»

Antithesis Economic relations in the non-material sphere of economics—indicated as—«bi»

Synthesis   Complex (joint) economic relations, which we will put down in the following way: $Z = a + bi$

Where—i—is a symbol reflecting the fact that these economic relations are realized on the «field» of non-material values (services)

The formula $Z = a + bi$ can written in the following vector form:

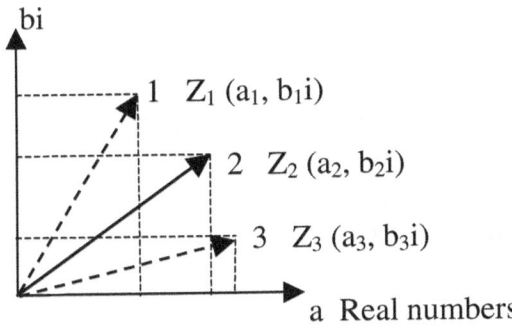

Vector Z_1—is situated above the bisector that means that in the social organism economic relations in the area of non-material values—services prevail;

Vector Z_2—coincides with the bisector of the angle and reveals the balanced ratio between economic relations which are realized both in the area of material values and non-material values—services;

Vector Z_3—which is situated lower than the bisector of the angle, reveals that social economic relations mostly take place in the area of material values and less in the area of non-material values—services.

If we use this kind of approach as regards relatively autonomous spheres of social production, the structure of economic relations becomes brighter and colorful.

We should not study the technology of making material and non-material products of human labor. The subject of political economy is not concerned with physical, chemical, or biochemical processes but only with economic relations, which arise between people during the process of production, distribution, exchange and consumption of values and services.

But we have to understand what kind of economic relations form between people as regards material and non-material values.

Related to this, one of the main problems which exists in the economics of the Internet sphere is as follows:

1. To reveal economic relations regarding Internet values—material results of activity—computers, software;
2. To reveal economic relations regarding Internet services—non-material results of activity;
3. To reveal the idea of complex economic relations in the Internet sphere.

The different nature of origin of Internet products (material and services) introduces special nuances into economic relations.

It is also obvious that the different nature of origin of Internet values and Internet services leaves that kind of special mark that can hardly be missed.

If Internet services reveal themselves in non-material form, economic relations that serve this type of product should be classified as— economic relations connected with non-material products of the Internet sphere.

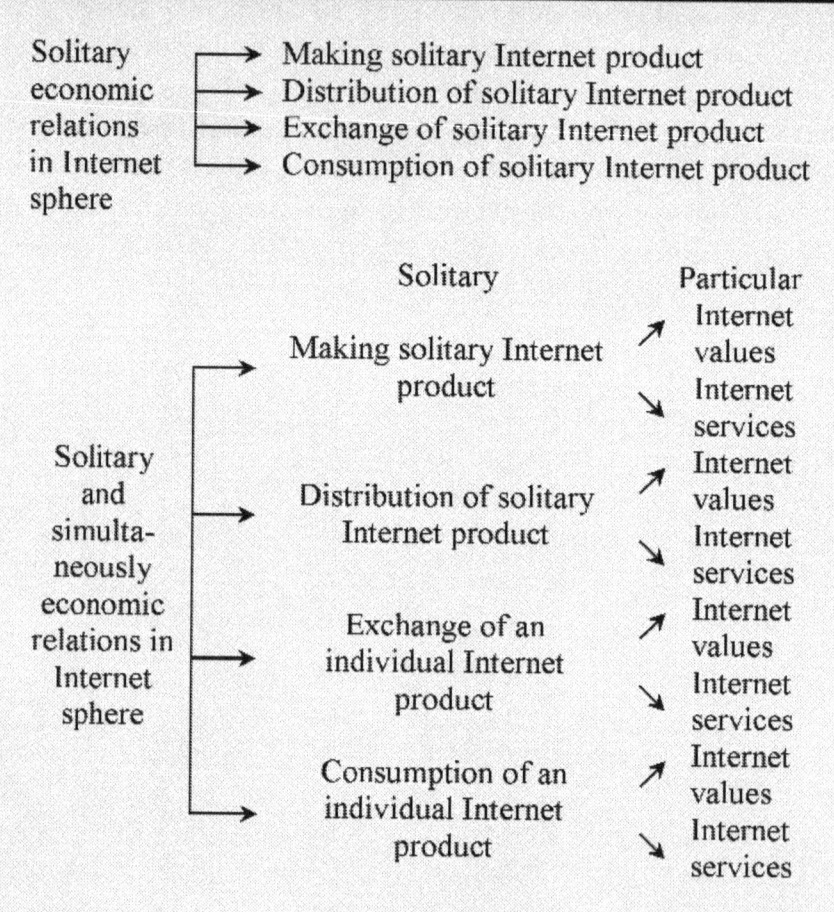

From the above complex economic relations in the Internet sphere, the following structure is revealed:

1) Structure of the relation of «creation» of Internet product

Thesis   Economic relations within which Internet values are made (real numbers)—«a_1»

Antithesis   Economic relations within which Internet services are made (imaginary numbers)—«$b_1 i$»

Synthesis   Complex economic relations within which joint Internet products are made (complex numbers $Z_1 = a_1 + b_1 i$)

2) For the «distribution» of the Internet product the following structure will be recorder:

Thesis   Real economic relations of «distribution» in the Internet sphere in the frame of which Internet values are distributed—material results (real numbers—«a_2»)

Antithesis   Imaginary economic relations of «distribution» in Internet sphere in the frame of which Internet services are distributed—non-material results of activity (imaginary numbers—«$b_2 i$»)

Synthesis   Complex economic relations of «distribution» in Internet sphere in the frame of which an Internet product having material and non-material components is distributed:
$Z_2 = a_2 + b_2 i$

3) For the economic relations of «exchange» of the Internet product the following structure will be recorder:

Thesis	Real economic relations of an «exchange» in the Internet sphere in the frame of which Internet values are exchanged—material results (real numbers—«a_3»)
Antithesis	Imaginary economic relations of an «exchange» in the frames of which Internet services are exchanged—non-material; results of activity (imaginary numbers—«b_3i»)
Synthesis	Complex economic relations of an «exchange» in Internet sphere in the frames of which an Internet product of material and non-material components is exchanged: $Z_3 = a_3 + b_3i$

4) For the economic relations of «consumption» of the Internet product the following structure will be recorder:

Thesis	Real economic relations of «consumption» in the Internet sphere in the frames of which Internet values are consumed—material results (real numbers—«a_4»)
Antithesis	Imaginary economic relations of «consumption» in Internet sphere in the frames of which Internet services are consumed—non-material results of activity Imaginary numbers—«b_4i»)
Synthesis	Complex economic relations of «consumption» in Internet sphere in the frames of which an Internet product of material and non-material components is consumed: $Z_4 = a_4 + b_4i$

Generally economic relations in Internet sphere will be as follows:
$$Z_1 = a_1 + b_1 i; Z_2 = a_2 + b_2 i; Z_3 = a_3 + b_3 i; Z_4 = a_4 + b_4 i.$$

5) For the relations of «ownership» the following structure will be recorded:

Thesis	Real relations of «ownership» in the Internet sphere in the frames of which Internet values—material results (real numbers—«a») are consumed
Antithesis	<u>Imaginary relations</u> of «ownership» in the Internet sphere in the frames of which Internet services non-material results of activity (imaginary numbers—«bi») are consumed
Synthesis	Complex relations of «ownership» in the frame of which an Internet product of material and non-material components are consumed (material and non-material parameters: $Z = a + bi$).

STRUCTURE OF THE ECONOMIC RELATIONS AND RELATIONS «OWNERSHIP» CONNECTED TO INTERNET VALUES

A) FIRST RELATION «PRODUCTION»

Production of Internet values

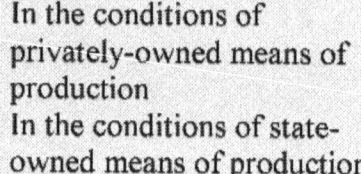

In the conditions of privately-owned means of production

In the conditions of state-owned means of production

B) SECOND RELATION «DISTRIBUTION»

Distribution of Internet values

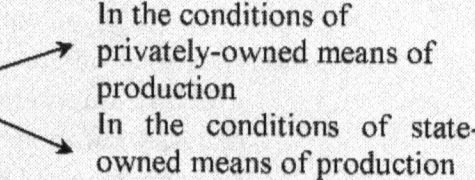

In the conditions of privately-owned means of production

In the conditions of state-owned means of production

C) THIRD RELATION «EXCHANGE»

Exchange of Internet values

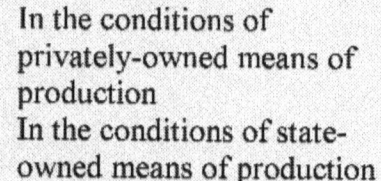

In the conditions of privately-owned means of production

In the conditions of state-owned means of production

D) FOURTH RELATION «CONSUMPTION»

Consumption of Internet values

In the conditions of privately-owned means of production

In the conditions of state-owned means of production

STRUCTURE OF THE ECONOMIC RELATIONS AND RELATIONS «OWNERSHIP» CONNECTED TO INTERNET SERVICES

A) FIRST RELATION «PRODUCTION»

Production of Internet services →

- In the conditions of privately-owned means of production
- In the conditions of state-owned means of production

B) SECOND RELATION «DISTRIBUTION»

Distribution of Internet services →

- In the conditions of privately-owned means of production
- In the conditions of state-owned means of production

C) THIRD RELATION «EXCHANGE»

Exchange of Internet services →

- In the conditions of privately-owned means of production
- In the conditions of state-owned means of production

D) FOURTH RELATION «CONSUMPTION»

Consumption of Internet services →

- In the conditions of privately-owned means of production
- In the conditions of state-owned means of production

STRUCTURE OF THE ECONOMIC RELATIONS AND RELATIONS «OWNERSHIP» CONNECTED TO INTERNET PRODUCT

A) FIRST RELATION «PRODUCTION»

Production of Internet product

→ In the conditions of privately-owned means of production

↘ In the conditions of state-owned means of production

B) SECOND RELATION «DISTRIBUTION»

Distribution of Internet product

→ In the conditions of privately-owned means of production

↘ In the conditions of state-owned means of production

C) THIRD RELATION «EXCHANGE»

Exchange of Internet product

→ In the conditions of privately-owned means of production

↘ In the conditions of state-owned means of production

D) FOURTH RELATION «CONSUMPTION»

Consumption of Internet product

→ In the conditions of privately-owned means of production

↘ In the conditions of state-owned means of production

The reader, certainly, will ask the question: What is the essence of general economic relations in the Internet sphere?

If we take into account every thing mentioned above and to the economic relations of making Internet values and services, distribution, exchange and consumption expenses we add «expenses», «incomes» «economic interests», «taxes» as well as melodies of «country» music, then to switch on all this at one time and then launch it all—that will be general (complex) economic relations in the Internet sphere.

3. COMPLEX CORRELATION OF FACTORS IN THE INTERNET SPHERE

For many years mathematicians had been working out a theory of complex numbers. In their research they tried to draw their abstract truths as near as possible to our everyday life. And they managed to do it because the logic of construction of these numbers, correspond to the logic of life, the logic of complex processes let it be in chemistry, biology or economics.

This logic is based on the following. In complex processes:
   – on the one hand there is a positive process;
   – on the other hand there is a negative process.

These two processes two sides constitute the essence of the whole combined, complex process.

This is how it happens in life. This is the truth you cannot ignore. It exists with us and without our will. The truth of processes: chemical, biological, and economic.

If we follow these two examples of logic: logic of life and logic in a complex number we will easily see that these kinds of logic do not differ. This is one and the same logic.

With the use of it we shall formalize the process of interaction of productive forces and economic relations:

Thesis   Productive force—material component of the process—«a»

Antithesis Economic relations in the frame of which productive force—non-material component of the process is functioning—«bi»

Synthesis   Interaction of (productive force and economic relations)—this complex process will be formalized and written as follows: $Z = a + bi$

Mark «i» reveals the fact that the nature of origin of productive forces is the same. Economic relations have the other nature of origin—non-material.

Productive forces and economic relations are different as regards the nature of their origin: the first component is material and the second non-material.

You cannot touch economic relations with your hands. These relations are non-material. Economic relations do not act as a material component, it is obvious. But at the same time they apply both to the field of «material» values and «non-material» values (services).

INTERNET SPHERE AS AN ECONOMIC SYSTEM

A) FIRST SUBDIVISION OF THE INTERNET SPHERE

To create computers and software people interact in economic relations. These relations are «the linking ether», which connects all factors of this particular process:
  — tools of the first subdivision of Internet sphere;
  — objects of labor of the first subdivision of Internet sphere;
  — labor resources of the first subdivision of Internet sphere.

Using the dialectical method, the logic of the complex number we shall write down the correlation of productive forces of the first subdivision of the Internet sphere and the economic relations, which exist in this part of the Internet sphere:

Thesis   Productive forces of the first subdivision of the Internet sphere—«a»

Antithesis   Economic relations in the first subdivision of the Internet sphere—«bi»

Synthesis   Interaction $Z = a + bi$

This scheme can be written as follows:

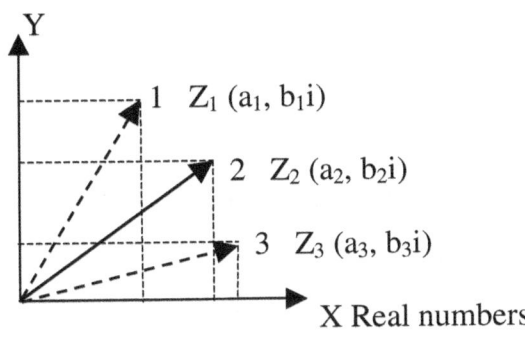

Position of vector 1—reveals that economic relations restrain development of productive forces «a» of the first subdivision of Internet sphere (rigid taxation).

Position of vector 2 coinciding with the bisector of the angle reveals the moderate restraint of development of productive forces of the first subdivision of the Internet sphere.

Position of vector 3 reveals that productive forces of the first division of the Internet sphere are developing under the conditions of limited restraint (preferential taxation, etc).

B. SECOND SUBDIVISION OF THE INTERNET SPHERE

Creation of Internet services presupposes the entering of people, or better to say, labor recourses into economic relations. Without these relations that are some kind of connecting links, it is impossible to create anything without these relations the following elements.[3]

Would remain in indefinite condition. But as soon as the above listed factors are engaged in the economic relations everything falls into place.

Using the logic of dialectical method, we will write down correlation of productive forces of the second subdivision of the Internet sphere and the economic relations, which exist in this part of the sphere.

Complex Internet written form the second subdivision of the Internet sphere—as an economic system:

---

[3] – tools of the second subdivision of the Internet sphere;

– objects of labor of the second subdivision of the Internet sphere;

– labor recourses of the second subdivision of the Internet sphere.

Thesis   Productive forces of the second subdivision of the
              Internet sphere—«a»

Antithesis   Economic relations of the second subdivision of the
              Internet sphere—«bi»

Synthesis   Interaction $Z = a + bi$

Graphic interpretation

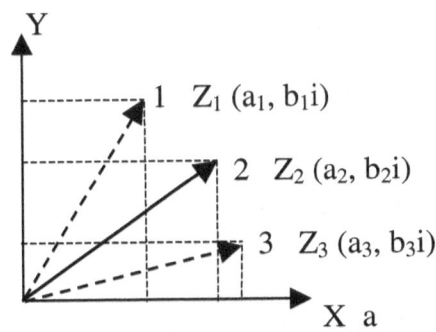

Y

1 $Z_1\ (a_1, b_1i)$

2 $Z_2\ (a_2, b_2i)$

3 $Z_3\ (a_3, b_3i)$

X a

Position of vector 1 reveals that economic relations restrain develop-
    ment of productive forces «a» of the second subdivision of the
    Internet sphere (rigid taxation).

Position of vector 2 coinciding with the bisector of the angle reveals the
    moderate restraint of development of productive forces of the
    second subdivision of the Internet sphere,

Position of vector 3 reveals that productive forces of the second subdivi-
    sion of the Internet sphere are developing under conditions of
    limited restraint (preferential taxation and etc).

C. COMPLEX VIEW: INTERNET SPHERE AS ECONOMIC SYSTEM

Internet sphere generally will be written as follows:

A. Complex correlation of factors in the first subdivision of Internet sphere

Thesis   Productive forces of the first subdivision of the Internet sphere—«a»

Antithesis Economic relations in the first subdivision of the Internet sphere—«bi»

Synthesis   Interaction Z = a + bi

B. Complex correlation of factors in the second subdivision of the Internet sphere

Thesis   Productive forces of the second subdivision of the Internet sphere—«a»

Antithesis Economic relations in the second subdivision of the Internet sphere—«bi»

Synthesis   Interaction Z = a + bi

C. Complex correlation of factors of a cumulative Internet process.

Thesis   Complex productive forces of the Internet sphere—«a»
Antithesis Complex economic relations of the Internet sphere—«bi»
Synthesis   Interaction Z = a + bi

Joint consideration of productive forces and economic relations existing in the Internet sphere—is the only correct approach. This is a complex approach.

CHAPTER 3. «REAL» AND «IMAGINARY» ECONOMIC PROPERTIES OF THE INTERNET PRODUCT

1. «REAL» AND «IMAGINARY» USE VALUE OF COMPLEX INTERNET PRODUCT

2. «REAL» AND «IMAGINARY» COST OF COMPLEX INTERNET PRODUCT

3. «REAL» AND «IMAGINARY» EXCHANGE VALUE OF COMPLEX INTERNET PRODUCT

Analysis of the literature on the economic problems of the Internet
sphere shows that until the present day the primary economic
proposes of its development have not been formulated yet. It is
still not clear what must prevail in the activity of Internet sphere:
Internet values[4] or Internet services?[5]

Economic properties of Internet values and Internet services have not
been considered in economic literature.

We do not know what Internet values and services are from an economic point of view.

Economic theory does not describe these categories properly.

The economic coordinates of these categories are unknown. It is still
not clear what remains on axis «X» and on axis «Y».

The time has come to make the first steps concerning this subject.

The difficulty of working out the economic problems of the Internet
sphere is that along with the comprehensible processes taking
place in computer and software producing fields, and where the
structure of costs and results, and the ratio of expenses and results
are clear there are Internet branches creating services and where it
is not clear what represents a result. What kind of criteria should
we use here: economic, social or something else?

In the beginning it is necessary to draw a line between Internet values
and services. If the area of application of real numbers is connected to and fixed with non-material values (services) of some
other origin, different from material ones, the result of such combination would be:

---

[4] Material values
[5] Non-material values

Thesis	Material Internet values—real numbers
Antithesis	Non-material Internet services—imaginary numbers
Synthesis	Complex Internet product—complex numbers

The logic of the general goal of the Internet sphere can be shown as:

Thesis	Economic aim of development of the first subdivision of the Internet sphere—Internet values—«a»
Antithesis	Economic aim of development of the second subdivision of the Internet sphere—Internet services—«bi»
Synthesis	Complex aim of development of the Internet sphere as a whole (taking into consideration the goals of development of the first and second subdivisions) $Z = a + bi$

Were index «i» reveals heterogeneity of products, their material and non-material character.

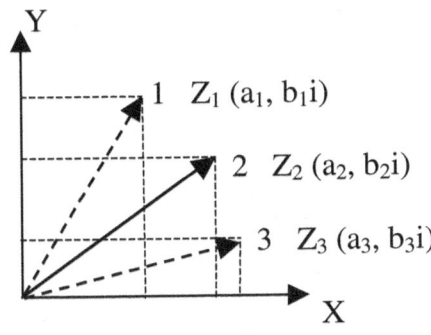

The graphic interpretation of the problem makes it possible to see that in case material Internet values prevail in the complex aim of the Internet sphere, Vector Z takes position Z_1.

In case non-material Internet values prevail, Vector Z takes the position Z_3.

In case of balanced development of the first and second subdivisions of the Internet sphere, complex aim of its development will coincide with the bisector of the angle φ, position 2 (Z_2).

Application of complex numbers is also necessary in calculating the expenditures of Internet products. You can see that expenditures are dual as regards their internal logic.

DIALECTIC LOGIC OF FORMING LABOR EXPENSES (WITH THE APPLICATION OF COMPLEX NUMBERS)

Thesis   Expenses of past labor (real numbers)
Antithesis Expenses of direct labor (imaginary numbers)
Synthesis   Aggregate labor expenses (complex numbers)

Graphic interpretation of forming expenses is as follows:

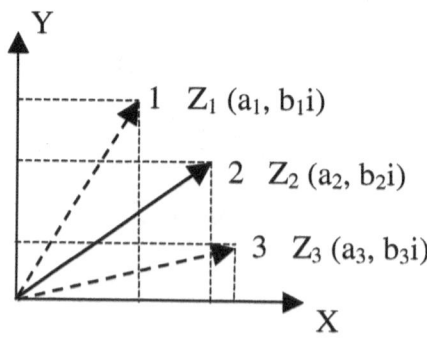

Vector Z_1—reveals that in the complex Internet product there are higher direct labor expenses than past labor expenses;

Vector Z_3—reveals an opposite situation: the complex Internet product has higher past labor expenses than that direct labor expenses.

Having read several pages of the book you will see that we cannot do without complex numbers. We need them during the calculations of both expenses and results of the Internet sphere.

1. «REAL» AND «IMAGINARY» USE VALUE OF COMPLEX INTERNET PRODUCT

1) USE VALUE OF INTERNET VALUES

Internet values are able to save their existence in a period of time between production and consumption. They can circulate during some time as products valid for sale.

The peculiarity of consumer properties of the Internet values of computers and software is that their significance is defined by how they satisfy productive, personal and eventually complex needs of the society.

If we consider the whole complex of Internet values, we will see that some of them act as economic values if somebody purchases them. But some Internet values, which do not represent themselves in that way, are not economic.

For better understanding of this topic let us use a graphic interpretation. Economic Internet values are placed on the X axis while non-economic Internet ones are set on the Y axis. The former can be interpreted graphically in the following way:

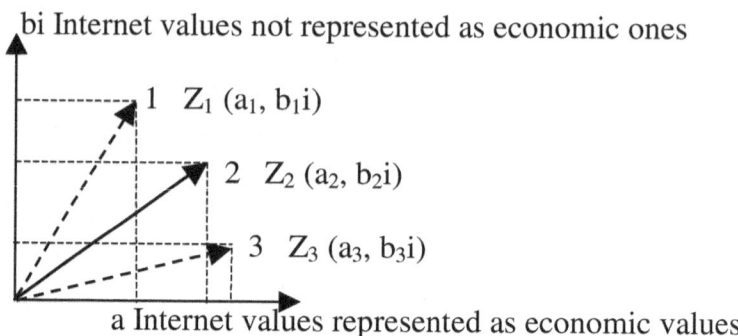

bi Internet values not represented as economic ones

1 Z_1 (a_1, b_1i)

2 Z_2 (a_2, b_2i)

3 Z_3 (a_3, b_3i)

a Internet values represented as economic values

Position of Vector Z_1—reveals that more than half of the Internet values do not represent economic ones.

Position of Vector Z_2—reveals that 50% of Internet values are represented as economic ones and 50% are not.

Position of Vector Z_3 shows that there are more Internet values represented as values than those which are not.

2) USE VALUE OF INTERNET SERVICES

Internet services have particular consumer properties. They are of different quality. They are represented as economic if they are the products of labor for others. They satisfy a definite part of productive, personal and complex needs of the society.

With the consumer properties of the Internet services there are a number of questions to answer:

First: it is difficult to <u>ascertain the consumer properties of Internet services before they have been consumed</u>.

Second: you can judge the quality of an Internet service only after it has been provided.

Here it is necessary to point out that if the recourse of the <u>working hours and online time—OLT</u> is not covered by Internet services, it means that the services do not exist. They are not consumed. Only in case of assimilation of recourse A_{STP}, Internet services are created and consumed. Here is one criterion:

Internet Service	+	A_{STP}	=	Use properties of Internet service

From these criteria it is seen that consumer characteristics of Internet services will be different depending on its second parameter:
- if a big quantity of OLT is assimilated, Internet services are of high consumer characteristics;
- if assumed recourse OLT, as they say, is moving to zero, <u>Internet services are of a low quality.</u>

Internet services are consumed during <u>working hours and spare time</u>. This is the functional peculiarity of Internet services: productive and personal—non-productive purpose. Complex numbers help formalize the various natures of consumption of Internet services. The former can be graphically interpreted in the following way:

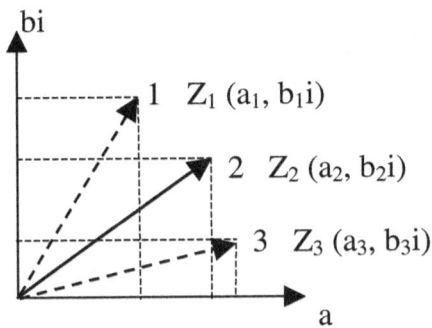

Where on axis «X»   Internet services consumed by population
                     at work—a—(economic services)

   on axis «Y»   Internet services consumed by population
                     during spare time—b (economic services)

   vector «Z»   Complex Internet services existing in the
                     market: $Z = a + bi$

Position of Vector Z_1 proves that more Internet services are consumed during spare time than during work time.

Position of Vector Z_2 reveals the division of the whole extend of
   Internet services:

   - 50% at a workplace during work hours;
   - 50% during spare time.

Position of Vector Z_3 shows that in a total amount of Internet
   services are created more at workplaces than during spare
   time.

3) «REAL» AND «IMAGINARY» USE VALUE OF A COMPLEX INTERNET PRODUCT

Use value of Internet value and Internet services means that they are
   beneficial for people, satisfy the demands of personal of productive character.

«Use value» of a complex Internet product is made:

   First: as a result of interaction of special factors of the working
      process:

      – means of work, tools, object of work, labor recourse—
         these create use value of Internet values.

Second: as a result of interaction of special factors of the service
process of work:
  a) in the process of «influencing» people with special
    means and tools the use value of Internet service is
    formed;
  b) <u>plus consumer properties of the «ASTP» resource assim-
    ilated by Internet services.</u>

Third: <u>complex real labor</u> in the Internet sphere creates definite
    Internet values and services having concrete consumer
    properties <u>plus consumer properties of the «OLT» recourse
    «OLT» assimilated by Internet services.</u>

The above said can be graphically interpreted in the following way:

Consumer properties of Internet services + OLT.

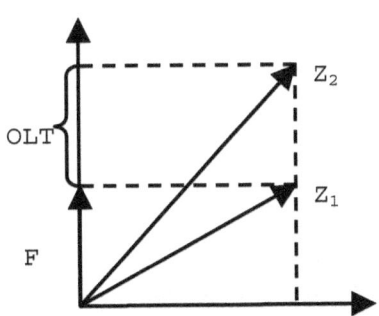

Consumer properties of Internet values

F—expenses of creating Internet values

It is seen from the diagram that consumer properties of the complex Internet product revealed by Vector Z_2, are joined by the use value of recourse OLT, assimilated by Internet services.

The graphic reveals that real use value of Internet product refer:
- use properties of Internet values—«a»

To imaginary use value of Internet product refer:—use properties of Internet services adjusted for OLT (bi = (F + OLT)i).

2. «REAL» AND « IMAGINARY» COST OF COMPLEX INTERNET PRODUCT

The Internet product is a composite phenomenon. It is comprised of Internet values and Internet services which act in two forms:
- Internet values:
    - a) natural form;
    - b) cost form.

- Internet services:
    - a) natural form;
    - b) cost form.

The cost of Internet values and Internet services are two big issues which can be considered either separately or together. There are many problems in this subject. Here it is necessary to specify the methods of research and the system of calculation.

How shall we sum up Internet values in material form with Internet services in their non-material form?

How can we make an elementary economic operation of «subtraction» of non-material Internet services from material Internet values?

These problems are necessary to be solved. To that end if we measure the cost of Internet values by axis «X» and cost of Internet service by axis «Y», the graphic will be:

«Y» Cost of Internet services (including cost «OLT»)

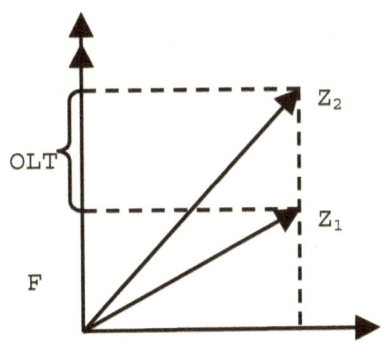

Cost of Internet values «X»

Vector $Z_1 = a_1 + b_1i$—reveals that cost of OLT recourse is not included in the cost of the complex Internet product.

Vector $Z_2 = a_2 + b_2i$—shows the inclusion of OLT resource into the cost of an Internet product.

In connection with the fact that OLT resource consists of two reciprocally opposite components:

a) work hours of OLT users;

b) online time of the users, Internet services OLTj, then a cumulative cost of a complex Internet product will be written in three-dimensional space:

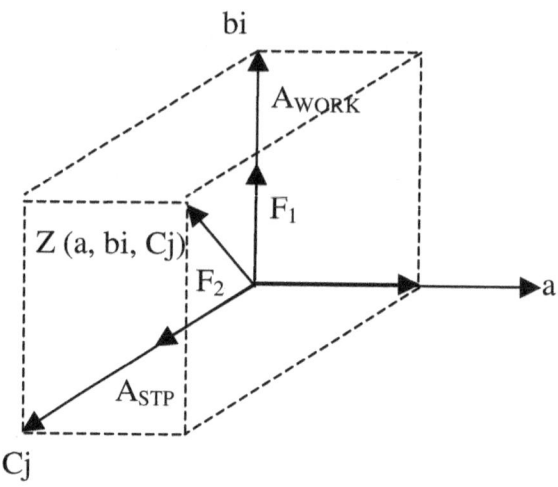

Cumulative Vector Z which reflect the cost of complex Internet product
with a resource $(A_{WORK} + A_{STP}) = OLT = (OLTi + OLTj)$ in
three-dimensional space is written as follows:

− $Z = a + bi + Cj$;[6]
− a—cost of Internet values «X»;
− bi—cost of Internet services $bi = (F_1 + A_{WORK})i$;
− Cj—cost of Internet services $Cj = (F_2 + A_{STP})j$;
− A_Fj—spare time of the users of Internet services.

F_1—expenses on Internet services of productive character;
F_2—expenses on Internet services of non-productive character;

$$R_{COMP} = a + (F_1 + A_{WORK})i + (F_2 + OLT)j$$

---

[6] Mathematicians call these numbers as super complex or quanterions.

3. «REAL» AND «IMAGINARY» EXCHANGE VALUES OF COMPLEX INTERNET PRODUCT

The economic utility of an Internet product is defined by its characteristics through which it satisfies the needs of people. This fact makes it a use value.

This problem has two sides, which should always be kept in mind. Internet values and services can become values if they are intended for exchange. The use value of goods must not satisfy the needs of the one who produced it, but placed on the market for consumption by other people through exchange thus satisfying the needs of other members of society.

Exchange value—is a quantitative relation in which use values of one kind are exchanged for use values of another kind. Their exchange value is conveyed in this quantitative relation of exchangeable values. The economic Internet values and services in certain quantities match each other on the basis of labor expenditures. The use value of different Internet values are quantitatively diverse and quantitatively inadequate but are similar as regards the expenditures.

In other words both Internet values and services are heterogeneous on the one hand and they are similar on the basis of expenditures so they can be exchanged in certain proportions.

The ability of some values or services to exchange with other ones in certain proportions define the idea of the «exchange value» category. [7]

---

[7] Any item of goods potentially possesses economic characteristics, namely:
- use value
- cost value
- exchange value

Benefits and services are of diverse character. They are qualitively inadequate. But since production costs occur in both cases there in some ground for exchange.

The characteristics, which allow the exchange for other values and services define the idea of the economic relation of «exchange».

1. Exchange of Internet values for other values and services:

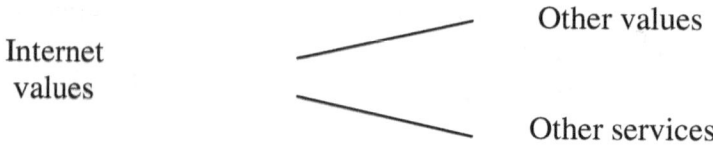

2. Exchange of Internet services for other values and services:

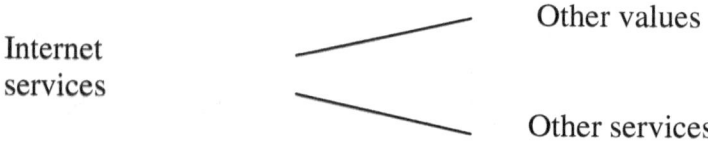

The exchange operations can be applied when the economic estimation
of Internet values corresponds to the economic estimation of
other values and services. These equalities occur in each relation
of an exchange where a certain coefficient is used.

The idea of the problem of «exchange» of Internet services for other
values and services is that consumption parameters of Internet
services have a significant range of variation.

Actually various combinations exist here:

- Internet service + OLT for school children;
- Internet service + OLT for college and university students;
- Internet service + OLT for industrial workers;
- Internet service + OLT for retired people.

Economic estimation regarding each variant will be different. In the first variant there will be one estimation. In the second one there will be other economic estimations etc.

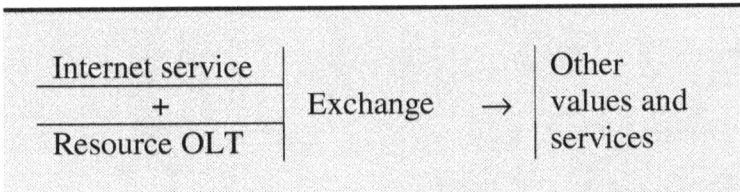

The final economic estimation of an Internet service can be established if there is knowledge of the assimilated oonline time resource of the population. On estimating this recourse economically it is possible to establish the final cost of an Internet service. Only after that it would be possible to specify the coefficient of exchange of an Internet service for other values and services.

The more OLT is assimilated the higher the amount of created Internet services. Is this in turn increases the volume of complex Internet product.

If we were to apply a thesis of a complex number, many unclear moments in the field of «exchange» relations of Internet values and services for other values and services become clear. Further on <u>we will give the detailed layout of relations of «exchange» in the Internet sphere with regard to complex numbers or it would be better to say that we will formalize relations of «exchange» using complex numbers.</u>

But here it is necessary to remember that an internal structure of expenses of an Internet product is complex too:

Thesis	Expenses of past labor at making Internet product—«a»
Antithesis	Expenses of direct labor at making Internet product—«bi»
Synthesis	Complex expenses of labor at making Internet product $Z = a + bi$

EXCHANGE OF AGGREGATE INTERNET PRODUCT FOR OTHER VALUES AND SERVICES

SPECIAL ECONOMIC RELATIONS IN THE INTERNET SPHERE		
A) Exchange of Internet values for other values and services with complex numbers		
Thesis Expenses of past labor in making Internet values—real number «a_1»	$\equiv$ coefficient $A_1{}^8$	Expenses of past labor in making values and services in other fields of production—real number «a_4»

---

[8] $\equiv$—Mark of identity

A.B.C.—coefficients of identity

Antithesis	Expenses of direct labor in making Internet values— imaginary number «b_1i»	$\equiv$ coefficient B_1	Expenses of direct labor in making values and services of other fields of production— imaginary number «b_4i»
Synthesis	Expenses of complex labor in making Internet values— complex number $Z_1 = a_1 + b_1i$	$\equiv$ coefficient C_1	Expenses of complex labor in making values and services of other spheres of production— complex number $Z_4 = a_4 + b_4i$

$$Z_1 \equiv Z_4 \times C_1$$
$$a_1 + b_1i \equiv (a_4 + b_4i)C_1$$

B) Exchange of Internet services with taking into account OLT resource for other values and services with complex numbers

Thesis	Expenses of past labor in making Internet values—real number «a_2»	$\equiv$ coefficient A_2[9]	Expenses of past labor in making values and services of other fields of production—real number «a_5»

---

[9] $\equiv$—Mark of identity
A.B.C.—coefficients of identity

Antithesis	Expenses of direct labor in making Internet values— imaginary number «b_2i»	$\equiv$ coefficient B_2	Expenses of direct labor in making values and services of other fields of production— imaginary number «b_5i»
Synthesis	Expenses of complex labor in making Internet values— complex number $Z_2 = a_2 + b_2i$	$\equiv$ coefficient C_2	Expenses of complex labor in making values and services of other spheres of production— complex number $Z_5 = a_5 + b_5i$

$$Z_2 \equiv Z_5 \times C_2$$
$$a_2 + b_2i \equiv (a_5 + b_5i)C_2$$

C) Exchange of Internet values and services with complex numbers

Thesis	Complex expenses of past labor in making Internet product (values and services) taking into account OLT resource—real number «a_3»	$\equiv$ coefficient A_3	Complex expenses of past labor in making values and services of other spheres of production—real number «a_6»

Antithesis	Complex expenses of direct labor in making Internet product (values and services) taking into account OLT resource—real number «a_3»	$\equiv$ coefficient B_3	Complex expenses of direct labor in making values and services of other spheres of production—real number «a_6»
Synthesis	Complex expenses of cumulative labor in making Internet product, taking into account OLT resource—real number «a_3» $Z_3 = a_3 + b_3i$	$\equiv$ coefficient C_3	Complex expenses of cumulative labor in making values and services of other spheres of production—real number «a_6»—$Z_6 = a_6 + b_6i$

$$Z_2 \equiv Z_6 \times C_3$$
$$a_2 + b_2i \equiv (a_6 + b_6i)C_3$$

Coefficients situated next to the mark of identity ($\equiv$) can change depending on the quality of Internet services, material values and other services.

In the conclusion of this chapter we will write in general form the economic characteristics of Internet values and services.

Note^ record of number Z_3 is not quite correct, since Z_2 is the sum of two complex numbers: Z_1 and Z_2, each reflecting diversified processes.

In the first case, production of Internet values:

$$Z_1 = a_1 + b_1 i$$

In the second case: production of Internet services:

$$Z_2 = a_2 + b_2 i + C_2 j$$

Z_3—is a complex number of a new type that is called quaternion in mathematics. It consists of two different complex numbers Z_1 and Z_2

$$Z_3 = Z_1 + Z_2 = a_1 + b_1 i + a_2 + b_2 i + C_2 j$$

1. Thesis Concrete labor	→	Use value of Internet values	→	Exchange value of Internet values
Production expenses on Internet values	→	Cost of Internet values	→	$Z_1 = a_1 + b_1 i$
2. Antithesis Concrete labor	→	Use value of an Internet service taking into account OLT resource	→	Exchange value of Internet services taking into account OLT resource

Production expenses of Internet services	→	Cost of Internet services taking into account OLT resource	→	$Z_2 = a_2 + b_2i + C_2j$
3. Synthesis Concrete labor	→	Complex use value of Internet product taking into account OLT resource	→	Exchange cost of complex Internet product taking into account OLT resource
Production expenses of the complex Internet product	→	Complex cost of Internet product taking into account OLT resource	→	$Z_3 = (a_1 + a_2) + (b_1i + b_2i + cj)$

It is necessary to remember that coefficient will be of real as well as Imaginary character, as are operations with real, imaginary and complex numbers.

Diagram №

DIALECTIC STRUCTURE OF EXCHANGE VALUE OF AGGRE-GATE INTERNET PRODUCT TAKING INTO ACCOUNT OLT RESOURCE

Thesis   Exchange value of an Internet values
$$Z_1 = a_1 + b_1 i$$

Antithesis Exchange value of an Internet service taking into account OLT resource
$$Z_2 = a_2 + b_2 i + cj$$

Synthesis Aggregate exchange value of an Internet product taking into account OLT resource
$$Z_3 = (a_1 + a_2) + (b_1 i + b_2 i) + cj$$

Here it is necessary to remember that OLT corresponds to an imaginary part of Internet services.

Z_3—is a complex number of a new type—in mathematics they call it quaternion.

Shall we give this category a detailed consideration.

DUAL STRUCTURE OF THE ECONOMIC PROPERTIES OF INTERNET VALUES

Thesis   Use value of Internet values
Antithesis Cost of Internet values
Synthesis Exchange value of Internet values

DUAL STRUCTURE OF THE ECONOMIC PROPERTIES OF INTERNET SERVICES (TAKING INTO ACCOUNT OLT RESOURCE)

Thesis   Use value of an Internet service taking into account OLT resource

Antithesis   Cost of an Internet service taking into account OLT resource

Synthesis   Exchange value of an Internet service taking into account OLT resource

DUAL STRUCTURE OF THE ECONOMIC PROPERTIES OF INTERNET PRODUCT (TAKING INTO ACCOUNT OLT RESOURCE)

Thesis   Complex use value of an Internet product, taking into account OLT resource

Antithesis   Complex cost of an Internet product, taking into account OLT resource

Synthesis   Complex exchange value of an Internet product, taking into account OLT resource

I proceed from the fact that a dual structure of Internet production suggests a dual structure of relations of exchange. This can be written as a logic scheme.

Table № 3.1

DIALECTIC STRUCTURE OF RELATIONS OF «EXCHANGE» IN THE INTERNET SPHERE TAKING INTO ACCOUNT OLT RESOURCE			
	THESIS	ANTITHESIS	SYNTHESIS
THESIS Relations of «exchange» in the first subdivision of IS into account OLT resource	Relations of «exchange» of means of labor and tools (past labor) in the first subdivision of IS taking into account OLT resource	Relations of «exchange» of manpower (direct labor) in the first subdivision of IS taking into account OLT resource	Relations of «exchange» of complex factors of production (past and direct labor) in the first subdivision IS taking into account OLT resource
ANTITHESIS Relations of «exchange» in the first subdivision of IS into account OLT resource	Relations of «exchange» of means of labor and tools (past labor) in the second subdivision of IS taking into account OLT resource	Relations of «exchange» of manpower (direct labor) in the second subdivision of IS taking into account OLT resource	Relations of «exchange» of complex factors of production (past and direct labor) in the second subdivision IS taking into account OLT resource
SYNTHESIS Relations of «exchange» in the first subdivision of IS into account OLT resource	Relations of «exchange» of means of labor and tools (past labor) in the first and second subdivision of IS taking into account OLT resource	Relations of «exchange» of manpower (direct labor) in the first and second subdivision of IS taking into account OLT resource	Relations of «exchange» of complex factors of production (past and direct labor) in the first and second subdivision IS taking into account OLT resource

CHAPTER 4. INTERNET ONLINE TIME

1. STREAM OF INTERNET VISITORS WITH TIME FACTOR TAKEN INTO ACCOUNT

The stream of visitors to the Internet is the primary, determinative resource of this sphere. If this flow ceased the whole of Internet activity would lose economic sense. Absence of stream of Internet visitors reduces Internet sphere services to zero.

The same apparently holds with all other aspects of economic relations within this area.

I suggest that visiting Internet be considered with the adjustment for time factor.

This would help to keep track of the dynamics and trends of the stream, to know the time when this resource is committed to economic relations or comes to a halt and stops participating in them. This is first.

Second, as soon as we engage the time factor we can see that the stream of the Internet visitors adjusted for the time component ceases to look like a «dried up» indicator. It acquires a shape and a volume. Time factor allows to establish extra parameters of the Internet visitors' flow.

And third. Visiting Internet with disregard of the time factor looks like single-dimentional static proportion. With it however we deal with two-or three dimentional measurement.

Apart from that if we subject the stream of Internet visitors to «logical separation» it will be divided into several layers of components.

    1. Visitors of the Internet during working hours. These are the ones using Internet services within working time;

    2. Visitors of the Internet in spare time

        a) part of the stream of visitors uses Internet services with the purpose of educational accomplishment;

        b) another part is aiming at enlightenment perfection;

        c) the rest of the Internet visitors are seeking for entertainment.

The above given classification of the Internet visitors stream in accordance with the functional quality makes it possible to proceed to clarification of the substance of a number of other economic categories.

2. INTERNET VISITOR'S TIME AS AN ECONOMIC RESOURCE

Until now online time (OLT) as an economic category has remained outside the research of the economists.

Why has it not been examined as an economic category?

Why has it not been studied as a resource like all other resources?

Is there a clearly defined structure of this resource, and if any, why has it not been established?

Are there any absolute and relative characteristics of it?

Why don't we know what causes the shortening of some of the time proportions and enlargement of the others?

Is online time resource (OLT) a part of «National Wealth», «National Property» «National Income», «Gross Domestic Product», «Net Domestic Product» or some other kind of complex indicator of social endeavor? However, all these questions remain unanswered.

One may avoid examining the stream of Internet visitors as an economic constituent of general flow of resource within the Internet sphere. Such a standpoint would, however, prompt of problems existing in the economy of the Internet sphere.

In my research I adhere to opposite presumptions—the stream of Internet visitors should be considered as an economic resource which needs to be estimated in terms of economy. This, as I have pointed out above, entails quite a number of unresolved questions. Their settlement depends only on our earnest inquisition.

Economic problems of the Internet sphere are directly connected to the «online time» resource. Internet services assimilate this specific resource in a large scale. In 2001 alone there were 150 million Internet users worldwide.

If each of them spent one hour a day consuming these services it would come to 150 million man-hours. Consumption of 8 hours per day would constitute 1.2 billion man-hours per day or 438 billion man-hours per year. This resource like any other one should be economically estimated.

Provided we have estimated one hour of the assimilated «online time» resource at 1 USD, total cost of the resource would make up 438 billion USD. If one hour of the above resource is estimated at 3 USD the total cost of it will reach 1.31 trillion USD. Below we shall examine this problem at a greater length.

The OLT resource as any other resource has the following economic characteristics:

- consumer characteristics;
- cost characteristics;
- exchange characteristics.

Without all these economic components the OLT resource under review cannot be on the same plane with other resources involved in the Internet sphere. It is obvious.

Economic estimation of the OLT resource should not be fragmented and provisional. It is an expensive resource demanding a relevant attitude.

The «online time» resource should be examined from the point of complex numbers, the logic that is used in the theory of complex numbers.

There is another reason to do it: an economic category—the «online time» resource—is feeble and one-sided when it is outside the logic of complex number. Examination of categories in the one-dimensional space looks banal and shallow. It is better not to consider them at all in a one-dimensional space. As regards the theory of complex numbers, an economic category—«online time» resource—gains two-dimensional and three-dimensional space.

3. «ONLINE TIME» RESOURCE AS A REAL PART OF THE WEALTH OF SOCIETY

In this part of the book we shall specify which part of the «online time» should be ascribed to a real component of society's wealth and which to an imaginary one.

To carry out an operation of «dismemberment» of the «online time» resource into real and imaginary parts, it is necessary to apply certain criteria.

These criteria, certainly, should be economic. I suggest that we use the following:

> It is widely known that an Gross Domestic Product includes the working hours of the production process.
>
> The time which remains behind the «gate of production», is not included in an internal gross product.
>
> If we apply the above logic to problems of the assimilated and non-assimilated part of the «online time» resource the judgment will be as follows:
>
> – assimilated part of the «online time» resource within Internet services should be related to an internal gross product;
>
> – there is no ground to include the non-assimilated part of «online time» resource in an internal gross product. It would look like working on a computer not connected to the Internet.

Establishing a border between <u>assimilated</u> and <u>non-assimilated</u> parts of the «online time» resource we, thus, establish:

– which part of the resource is included in the process of creating intellectual and Internet services;

– which part of the resource remains uncovered.

Graphically this concept can be shown as follows:

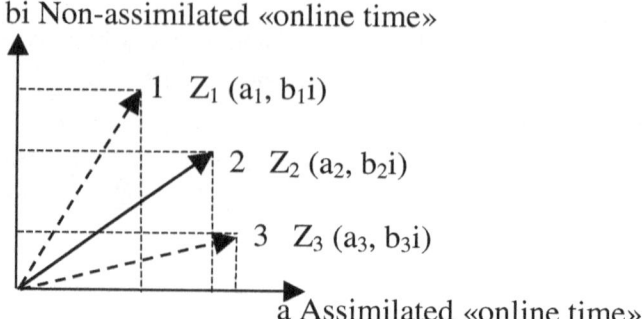

bi Non-assimilated «online time»

1 $Z_1 (a_1, b_1i)$

2 $Z_2 (a_2, b_2i)$

3 $Z_3 (a_3, b_3i)$

a Assimilated «online time»

Vector Z shows that there is more of the non-assimilated resource in aggregate «online time» than that of the assimilated one.

Vector Z coincides with the bisector of the angle, meaning that the assimilated OLT is equal to non-assimilated part of OLT.

In the graphic given above we consider «online time» resource from the position of complex numbers, i.e.:

Thesis   Assimilated OLT resource—real number—«a_1»

Antithesis Non-assimilated OLT resource—imaginary numbers—«b_1i»

Synthesis Aggregate «online time»—imaginary numbers (labor)—$Z = a_1 + b_1i$

Hence not all the «online time» resource of a person or society can be ascribed to the wealth, but only the part, which is involved in the service process. In other words the wealth of a society does not consist of the potential part of the «online time» but of the consumption part of an internal gross product in the process of an intellectual Internet service.

4. ONLINE TIME RESOURCE OF THE WORKING AND NON-WORKING PART OF THE POPULATION

Online time resource of the working and non-working part of the population are two different sides of the same resource. Such a functional distinction is needed for the reason of unequal cost of OLT resource. The unit of this resource for the working population is several times higher than economic qualities of a similar resource of the non-working population.

1. Economic characteristics of the «online time» resource of working part of population.

Thesis	Use value of human resource within «online time» resource of the working population
Antithesis	Cost of human resource within «online time» resource of the working population
Synthesis	Exchange value of human resource within «online time» resource of the working population

2. Economic characteristics of the «online time» resource of non-working part of population.

Thesis	Use value of human resource within «online time» resource of the non-working population
Antithesis	Cost of human resource within «online time» resource of the non-working population
Synthesis	Exchange value of human resource within «online time» resource of the non-working population

Both of the structures prove that:

1. Use value of the «online time» resource of the working part of the population is different from the use value of the similar resource among the non-working population;

2. Cost of the OLT resource of the working population is different from the use value of the similar resource of the non-working population;

3. Exchange value of the OLT resource of the working part of the population is different from the use value of the similar resource of the non-working population;

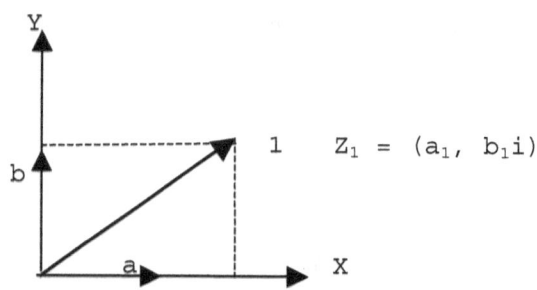

where

a_1—«online time» of the working population

b_1i—«online time» of the non-working population

$Z = a_1 + b_1i$—«online time» of both working and non-working parts of the population

The distinction between economic estimates of the online time resource involves certain corrections in the calculation of the Internet services cost.

Thus, for example, if the Internet visiting time is estimated at 438 billion man-hours per annum and if 85% of it falls on the economically developed countries, total amount of OLT there will make up:

438 X 0.85 = 372 billion man-hours.

Proceeding from the assumption that 50 % of OLT, i.e. 186 billion man-hours, is used for production needs, the remaining half will go to meet non-production requirements.

Also, if in the developed countries one working hour is estimated at 10 USD, 186 billion OLT hours will be evaluated at 1.86 trillion USD. Furthermore, one working hour estimated at 15 USD will raise the amount to 2.79 trillion USD.

The second part of the Internet visitors stream.

However cost evaluation of the Internet visitors stream during spare time cannot be estimated at 10-15 USD. It is several times less than that. If one hour of OLT spare time were to be estimated at 1 USD, then:

186 billion hours X 1USD = 0.186 trillion USD

If 1 hour of OLT = 2 USD, 186 billion hours X 2 USD = 0.372 trillion USD

If 1 hour of OLT = 3 USD, 186 billion hours X 2 USD = 0.558 trillion USD

The stream of Internet sphere visitors stipulates noticeable additions in the economic assessments.

Internet services are directed to the assimilation and maximum use of the «online time» resource by different groups of population.

We shall write down the assimilation criterion for the spare time of visitors to Internet:

$$\text{Criterion} = \frac{\text{OLT assimilated resource}}{\text{Expenses on OLT assimilated}}$$

Processes of assimilation of OLT necessary to be considered as:

- working part of population;
- non-working part of population.

COMPLEX APPROACH TO OLT ASSIMILATION
WORKING PART OF POPULATION

1. Thesis criterion

$$\frac{\text{Assimilation of «online time» resource of population (OLT)}}{\text{Past labor expenses (a) a real number}}$$

2. Antithesis criterion

$$\frac{\text{Assimilation of «online time» resource of population (OLT)}}{\text{Direct labor expenses (bi) an imaginary number}}$$

3. Synthesis criterion

$$\frac{\text{Assimilation of «online time» resource of population (OLT)}}{\text{Expenses of aggregate labor } (Z = a + bi) \text{ a complex number}}$$

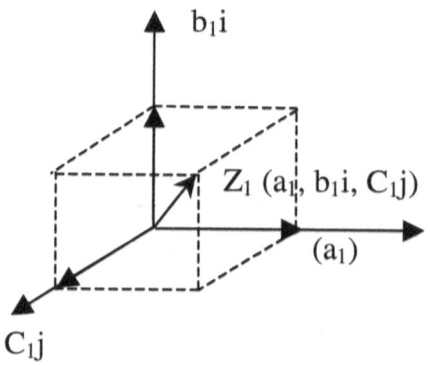

Where «a1»—direct labor expenses of assimilation of OLT resource working part of population;

«b1i»—past labor expenses of assimilation of OLT resource working part of population;

«C1j»—assimilated OLT resource working part of population.

COMPLEX APPROACH TO OLT ASSIMILATION NON-WORKING PART OF POPULATION

1. Thesis criterion

$$\frac{\text{Assimilation of «online time» resource of population (OLT)}}{\text{Past labor expenses (a) a real number}}$$

2. Antithesis criterion

$$\frac{\text{Assimilation of «online time» resource of population (OLT)}}{\text{Direct labor expenses (bi) an imaginary number}}$$

3. Synthesis criterion

$$\frac{\text{Assimilation of «online time» resource of population (OLT)}}{\text{Expenses of aggregate labor } (Z = a + bi) \text{ a complex number}}$$

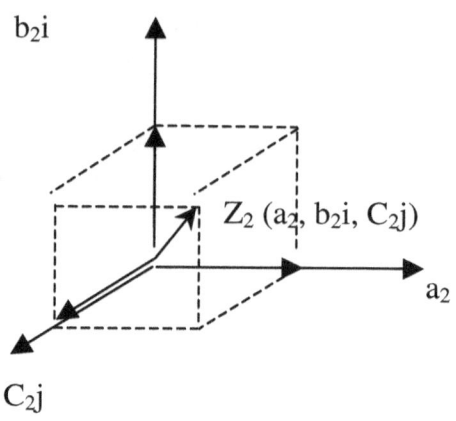

Where «a2»—direct labor expenses of assimilation of OLT resource non-working part of population;

«b2i»—past labor expenses of assimilation of OLT resource non-working part of population;

«C2j»—assimilated OLT resource non-working part of population.

Processes of assimilation of OLT necessary to be considered as:

- working part of population;

- non-working part of population.

5. THREE CONSTITUENT PARTS OF THE ASSIMILATED ONLINE TIME RESOURCE

OLT resource should be considered functionally, in different spheres:

- in a sphere of education;

- in a sphere of enlightenment;

- in a sphere of entertainment.

The problem of its assimilation has two aspects: educational and entertaining.

The above can be written down graphically:

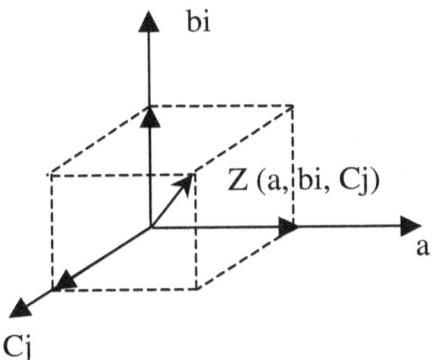

Where «a»—assimilation of OLT resource by the services of education;

«bi»—assimilation of OLT of enlightenment resource by industry services ;

«Cj»—assimilation of OLT of entertainment resource by industry services;

CHAPTER 5. «REAL», «IMAGINARY» AND «COMPLEX» ESTIMATION OF EXPENSES CONNECTED TO THE MOVEMENT OF THE INTERNET PRODUCT

1. SHORTCOMIINGS OF THE METHOD OF CALCU-
   LATING OF EXPENSES
   A) ANALOGY IN CALCULATING EXPENSES
   B) METHOD OF EXPENSES AND ECONOMIC
      RELATIONS
   C) METHOD OF CALCULATING OF EXPENSES
      IN THE INTERNET SPHERE

2. CLASSIFICATION OF EXPENSES CONNECTED
   TO THE MOVEMENT OF THE INTERNET
   PRODUCT
   A) BY MATERIAL CRITERIA
   B) BY SECOND CRITERIA

3. UTILIZATION OF COMPLEX NUMBERS IN ECO-
   NOMIC CALCULATIONS OF EXPENSES CON-
   NECTED TO THE MOVEMENT OF THE
   INTERNET PRODUCT WITHIN RELATIONS
   OF PRODUCTION

4. UTILIZATION OF COMPLEX NUMBERS IN ECO-
   NOMIC CALCULATIONS OF EXPENSES CON-
   NECTED TO THE MOVEMENT OF THE
   INTERNET PRODUCT WITHIN RELATIONS
   OF DISTRIBUTION

5. UTILIZATION OF COMPLEX NUMBERS IN ECO-
   NOMIC CALCULATIONS OF EXPENSES CON-
   NECTED TO THE MOVEMENT OF THE
   INTERNET PRODUCT WITHIN RELATIONS
   OF EXCHANGE

6. UTILIZATION OF COMPLEX NUMBERS IN ECO-
   NOMIC CALCULATIONS OF EXPENSES CON-
   NECTED TO THE MOVEMENT OF THE
   INTERNET PRODUCT WITHIN RELATIONS
   OF CONSUMPTION

1. SHORTCOMIINGS OF THE METHOD OF CALCULATING OF EXPENSES

A) ANALOGY IN CALCULATING EXPENSES

In the economic theory of material production it has taken many years to form the method of calculating expenses. It has been a long way with numerous mistakes and errors in calculations. Take for example the «Smith's dogma» according to which the value of the aggregate product is divided into earnings, profit and rent. According to Smith aggregate cost does not incorporate expenses of past labor. Such a specific point of view on expenses did not allow elaboration on many problems, e.g.: efficiency of usage of the resources and reproduction.

At present this method is being transferred to the other areas, such as intellectual, the Internet sphere, health, transport and military. In each of these areas there are many unclear issues related to the economic calculations of expenses.

Apart from it, the absence of necessary studies in the economic theory leads to the fact that there is a substitution of the criterion «result» by the criterion «expenses».

Especially in the areas producing non–material values, there is an attempt to increase expenses as if they try to show the society, that the volume of services in intellectual, the Internet, medical, transport and military area grows.

However the increase of expenses could also be a result of a low quality of the used resources, mistakes, errors or defeat on a battlefield.

It turns out that the higher expenses and the worse the functioning of the autonomous sphere, the better for the society. This is where the essence of the substitution of the criteria is expenses occur in the quality of a result.

The answer comes automatically: without through academic investigation, explanation of the economic peculiarities of the above spheres, mechanical transfer of the methods of calculating expenses, borrowed from material sphere would result in a noticeable number of logical mistakes.

B) METHOD OF EXPENSES AND ECONOMIC RELATIONS

If economic relations are looked upon as a solitary aspect, they resolve themselves into:
– solitary process of production
– solitary process of distribution
– solitary process of exchange
– solitary process of consumption

In the process of reproduction these relations fall into a certain chain.

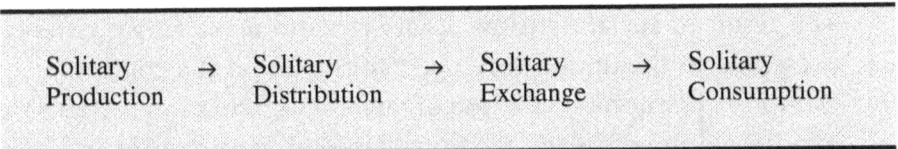

| Solitary Production | → | Solitary Distribution | → | Solitary Exchange | → | Solitary Consumption |

A product moves from one phase to the next. Its traffic is uninterrupted.

1) The movement of the product starts during production. Production is a process of creation of all possible values and services assigned for satisfying productive and personal needs. During the process of creating values and services, people step into economic relations, which act as an invisible connecting thread.

2) Distribution is the next step of the product movement. It is a necessary economic phase of the reproduction of the social product: material, intellectual, etc. It is an economic relation, which arises between people in the further movement of products of labor, from a producer to a consumer.

It is an economic relation, which considered it in its «pure» form, is located between production on the one hand, and exchange on the other. It includes the distribution of tools of labor, labor resources and products of labor. Distribution of collective social product is a point of departure of expanded reproduction that defines the proportions and pace of reproduction. Its character and principles depend on the legal system e.g.: law of ownership, etc.

3) Exchange is the next step of product's movement.

Exchange of products is a form of economic tie among people during which the product of labor (material or non–material) is exchanged simply and directly for another product of labor (material or non–material). An exchange of products originated as a result of social division of labor. Natural exchange has been preserved in the under-developed countries, in the conditions of economic disruption, collapse of currency circulation. Expansion and development of the relations based on commodity and currency exchange has been a necessary condition of transition from the barter exchange to the relations based on commodity and currency exchange.

Development of social division of labor has caused the transformation of barter into a permanent form of connection between private producers of goods.

In the conditions of developed commodity and currency relations, the phase of «exchange» is a mutual expropriation of products of labor. It is a phase of social reproduction connecting production and conditioned by it distribution on one side, and consumption on the other. The core of the exchange is the social division of labor. Exchange influences development of production.

The economic relations pertaining to the exchange of values and services has a specific place in the following chain:

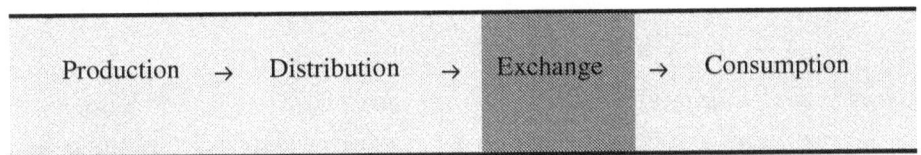

On one side of economic relations of «exchange» there is «distribution», on the other—«consumption». The necessity of defining the co–ordinates of «exchange» is not far-fetched. We should know what position it has and what it is surrounded by.

4) «Consumption» is the next step of the product's movement. It is an economic relation occurring between people in the production process (production consumption) and non–production consumption, i.e. personal consumption of values and services by the population.

Production consumption is included directly in the process of production and means usage of various means of production (such as plants, tools, fuels, raw materials etc) in this process.

Non–production consumption is a usage of various values and services by a man in order to satisfy his needs (food products, clothes, shoes, education, entertainment etc). Being dependent from production, consumption in turn influences production.

Chain of economic relations:

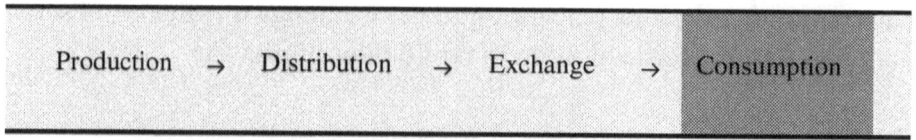

shows that if to analyze the relation of consumption in a pure form, it completes the entire system of economic relations. On the other hand, it serves as a link between production, distribution and exchange apart from that there are some conflicting points between production and consumption that can be solved in various ways and methods.

In economic literature the expense side of production is examined very scrupulously.

But at the same time within the relations of «distribution», «exchange» and «consumption» the aspect of expense is missing, it is put aside while investigating economic relations.

According to this logic, if we follow it, expenses within these three relations—distribution, exchange and consumption likely—are non–existent too.

But expenses exist, whether we want it or not.

This we can present in the following way:

Production		Distribution		Exchange		Consumption
Solitary «production»	→	Solitary «distribution»	→	Solitary «exchange»	→	Solitary «consumption»
↓		↓		↓		↓
Expenses of this kind of economic relations		Expenses of this kind of economic relations		Expenses of this kind of economic relations		Expenses of this kind of economic relations

Expenses should be considered in the context of each economic relation adjusted for material and non–material product.
- expenses connected to «production» of values;
- expenses connected to «production» of services;
- expenses connected to «distribution» of values;
- expenses connected to «distribution» of services;
- expenses connected to «exchange» of values;
- expenses connected to «exchange» of services;
- expenses connected to «consumption» of values;
- expenses connected to «consumption» of services.

On examining general problems connected to a category «expenses» we have to stress that this subject is also important in connection to the Internet sphere.

C) METHOD OF CALCULATING OF EXPENSES IN THE INTERNET SPHERE

One of the key issues of the Internet sphere is how to sum up material Internet values with that of non-material ones.

We will answer these problems when we find out the costs involved in the Internet sphere of production; what kind of structure they have, and whether all the resources involved in the production of Internet values and services are taken into account.

1. Calculation of expenses connected to the movement of an Internet product can be carried out by starting from the «narrow» point of view. This means that researchers examine only the service element of the Internet sphere and forget that there is a group of branches, which creates Internet values, computers and software, etc.

One shortcoming of calculating costs from this narrow point of view is
that researchers do not use a functional factor, which combines
the Internet branches into the so-called first division and second
division of this sphere.

2. The essence of the «wide» point of view is that a functional character
of the Internet sphere is taken into consideration. The sphere is
examined as an integral economic system, consisting of two parts:
  – the first division of the Internet sphere—the branches produc-
    ing Internet products: computers, software etc.
  – the second division of the Internet sphere—the branches, pro-
    ducing Internet services of enlightening, educational and
    show character.

In connection with this, calculation of Internet sphere «expenses»
should be performed for the whole integral economic system and
not for its components individually.

The logic of calculating the expenses of the Internet sphere will look
like:
  – expenses of producing Internet values;
  – expenses of producing Internet services;
  – aggregate expenses of producing Internet products.

Until the present day, in economic literature a category of costs has
been examined within a process of production of Internet values
and services but for all that researches (willingly of not) forget
about costs, which occur as the result of Internet product movement within the relations of distribution, exchange and consumption of Internet values and services.

In other words in the economic theory of the Internet we witness a «circus trick»: economic relations connected to distribution,
exchange and consumption of Internet values and services are
present, but the expenses of labor connected to these relations are

not taken into consideration. These expenses remain outside the field of vision of economists formulating the Internet sphere's economic theory.

Not only production of Internet values and Internet services are related to some kind of expenditure but also to their «distribution», «exchange» and «consumption». This is a given thing. «Expense» category cannot be surveyed detached from economic relations as well as economic relations without the expense part.

If economic relations were to be considered as an individual aspect with reference to the Internet sphere they would be reduced to:

– solitary process of producing Internet values and services;
– solitary process of distributing Internet values and services;
– solitary process of exchanging Internet services and values;
– solitary process of consuming Internet values and services.

During the process of reproduction these relations line up a certain chain.

Production	Distribution	Exchange	Consumption
Solitary «production» of Internet values and Internet services →	Solitary «distribution» of Internet values and Internet services →	Solitary «exchange» of Internet values and Internet services →	Solitary «consumption» of Internet values and Internet services

Within each of the economic relations there are specific expenses. The above can be written as follows:

Production	Distribution	Exchange	Consumption
Solitary «production» $\rightarrow$	Solitary «distribution» $\rightarrow$	Solitary «exchange» $\rightarrow$	Solitary «consumption»
$\downarrow$	$\downarrow$	$\downarrow$	$\downarrow$
Expenses of this kind of economic relations	Expenses of this kind of economic relations	Expenses of this kind of economic relations	Expenses of this kind of economic relations

Movement of Internet values and services from the producer to the consumer occurs at varying pace.

1. The way of movement of Internet values

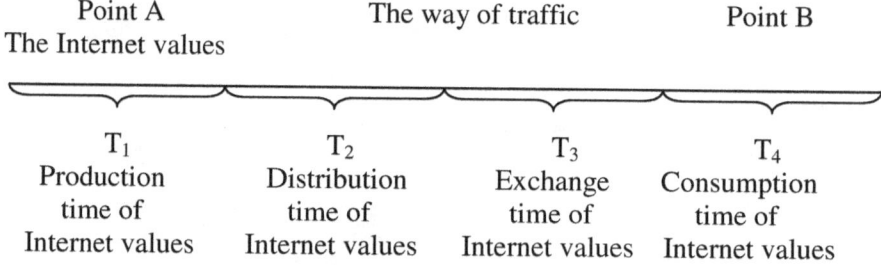

Point A The Internet values	The way of traffic		Point B
T_1 Production time of Internet values	T_2 Distribution time of Internet values	T_3 Exchange time of Internet values	T_4 Consumption time of Internet values

If we summarize these time intervals the entire moving time would be:
$$T = T_1 + T_2 + T_3 + T_4$$

The way of movement of Internet services

The peculiarity of Internet services is that their time of production, distribution, and exchange—coincides with the time of consumption.

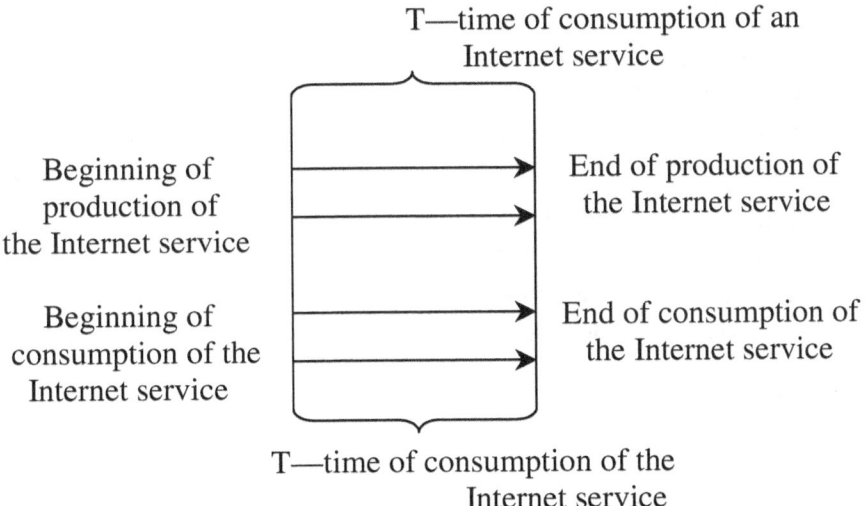

T—time of consumption of an
Internet service

Beginning of
production of
the Internet service

End of production of
the Internet service

Beginning of
consumption of the
Internet service

End of consumption of
the Internet service

T—time of consumption of the
Internet service

The peculiarity of the Internet service is that the process of its creation is accompanied by its consumption and distribution. All this occurs in a single interval of time. Schematically the above can be written as follows:

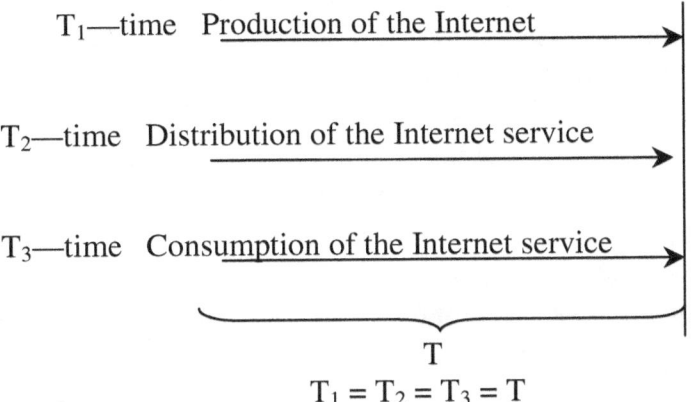

T_1—time Production of the Internet

T_2—time Distribution of the Internet service

T_3—time Consumption of the Internet service

T

$$T_1 = T_2 = T_3 = T$$

But here it would be necessary to remember that:

1) The <u>production time</u> has a dual structure:

    Thesis   The production time of Internet values
    Antithesis The production time of Internet services
    Synthesis The production time of an aggregate Internet product

2) The <u>distribution time</u> has a dual structure:
    Thesis   The distribution time of Internet values
    Antithesis The distribution time of Internet services
    Synthesis The distribution time of an aggregate Internet product

3) The <u>consumption time</u> has a dual structure:

    Thesis   The consumption time of Internet values
    Antithesis The consumption time of Internet services
    Synthesis The consumption time of an aggregate Internet product

At every stage of the movement of Internet services and values people become part of economic relations. At every stage of the movement of material and non–material Internet values and services there are expenses of past labor, direct labor and, aggregate labor.

If we examine the expenses separately from economic relations, a number of questions arise:

How should these expenses (of past and direct labor) be compensated for the recurrence of the complex process of production, distribution, exchange and consumption?

How would compensation of expenses be carried out as regards <u>production</u> of material and non-material parts of an Internet product?

How would compensation of expenses connected to the <u>distribution</u> of material and non–material parts of an Internet product be made?

How would the expenses related to the <u>exchange</u> of material and non–material parts of an Internet product be compensated?

How would they compensate the expenses connected to the <u>consumption</u> of material and non-material parts of an Internet product?

Economic relations exist within the movement of Internet values and services from a producer to consumer. Certainly, there are expenses connected to that movement.

There is no place of a kind of «circus tricks». Economic theory doest not permit them. Everything should respond to reality and be reflected in economic categories.

Aggregate scheme of movement of Internet values and Internet services can be written as follows:

Production	Distribution	Exchange	Consumption
Solitary «production» of Internet values →	Solitary «distribution» of Internet values →	Solitary «exchange» of Internet values →	Solitary «consumption» of Internet values
↓	↓	↓	↓
Expenses of this kind of economic relations →	Expenses of this kind of economic relations →	Expenses of this kind of economic relations →	Expenses of this kind of economic relations
Solitary «production» of Internet services →	Solitary «distribution» of Internet services →	Solitary «exchange» of Internet services →	Solitary «consumption» of Internet services
↓	↓	↓	↓
Expenses of this kind of economic relations →	Expenses of this kind of economic relations →	Expenses of this kind of economic relations →	Expenses of this kind of economic relations

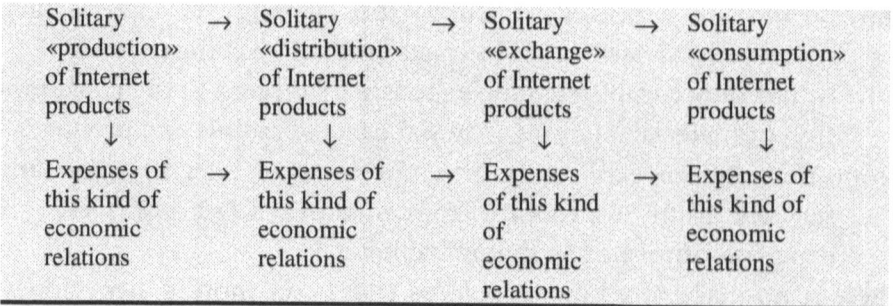

Solitary «production» of Internet products	→	Solitary «distribution» of Internet products	→	Solitary «exchange» of Internet products	→	Solitary «consumption» of Internet products
↓		↓		↓		↓
Expenses of this kind of economic relations	→	Expenses of this kind of economic relations	→	Expenses of this kind of economic relations	→	Expenses of this kind of economic relations

Hence there is only one conclusion: reproduction of the Internet sphere is possible provided all economic relations are implemented collectively on lack of these relations—production, distribution, exchange, and consumption. And if so, the expenses should also be examined.

2. CLASSIFICATION OF EXPENSES CONNECTED TO THE MOVEMENT OF THE INTERNET PRODUCT

A) BY MATERIAL CRITERIA

In the meantime new categories connected to the Internet sphere enter the science of economics: Internet values, Internet services, economic relations in Internet, and a new perception of the socially organized process of Internet sphere production.

In the first stages of investigating problems of the Internet sphere it would be necessary to classify expenses.

Let us consider a graphic interpretation of this criterion:

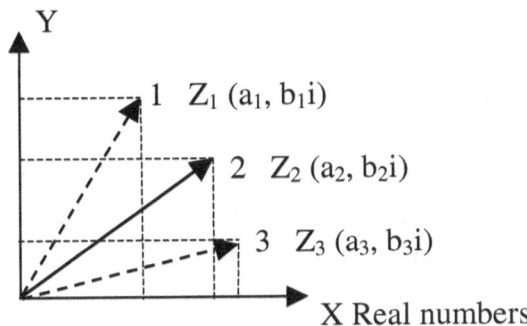

Expenses of Internet values (material), are set on the X axis and expenses of Internet services on the Y axis.

Vector Z shows aggregate, complex expenses concerning Internet values of the first and the second kind.

If Vector Z_1 is above the bisector of the angle φ, the expenses of the values of the second kind (non-material) are higher than those of the first kind.

If Vector Z_2 coincides with the bisector of the angle φ, the expenses of the values of the first and the second kinds are equal.

Position of the Vector Z_3 below the bisector of angle φ shows that the expenses of first kind values are much higher than those of the values of the second kind (non–material).

If we use a criterion of a «material» and «non–material» form of result the above allows us to classify expenses according to the various kinds of economic relations.

Calculation of expenses should be done separately on every aspect of economic relations: production, distribution, exchange and consumption (in the context of economic relations).

A material and non–material criterion should be applied within each economic relation: production, distribution, exchange and consumption.

- expenses connected to the «production» of Internet values;
- expenses connected to the «production» of Internet services;
- expenses connected to the «distribution» of Internet values;
- expenses connected to the «distribution» of Internet services;
- expenses connected to the «exchange» of Internet values;
- expenses connected to the «exchange» of Internet services;
- expenses connected to the «consumption» of Internet values;
- expenses connected to the «consumption» of Internet services.

Here there is every necessary thing to use simple and compound complex numbers:
- different nature of origin of economic relations;
- different nature of origin of Internet products: material and services (non-material).

1) If we arrange economic relations on coordinates «X», «Y», and «Z», on axis «X» we should set the expenses of «production» of an Internet product; on axis «Y»—the expenses of «distribution» of an <u>Internet product</u>; on axis «Z»—the expenses of «exchange» of an <u>Internet product</u>:

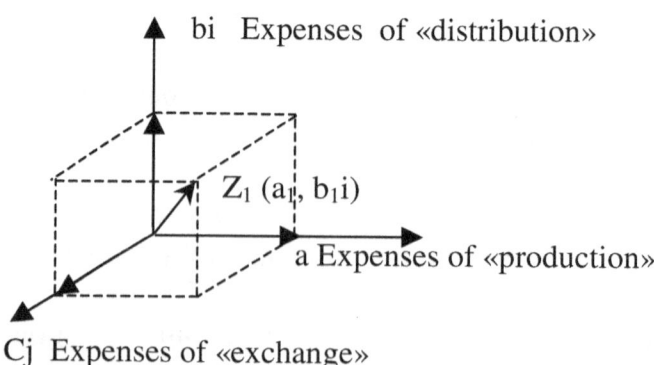

bi Expenses of «distribution»

$Z_1 (a_1, b_1 i)$

a Expenses of «production»

Cj Expenses of «exchange»

The total vector under these three economic vectors Z_1 will be written down as a compound complex number—quaternion.

$$Z_{123} = a + bi + cj$$

Where—a—a expenses of «production»;
   bi—a expenses of «distribution»;
   cj—a expenses of «exchange».

Imaginary units—i, j—reveal different (heterogeneous) nature of origin of economic relations.
If we proceed from that the chain of economic relations consists of:

Production	→	Distribution	→	Exchange	→	Consumption

The aggregate economic expenses will be written down as a complex number (quaternion)—the number increased by one more position.
$$Z_{1234} = a + bi + cj + pl$$

Where—p—is a expenses of «consumption»;
   1—is an imaginary unit.

Total Vector Z_{1234} will take different positions in the «economic sphere» depending on what kind of expenses will happen in each economic relation.

2) The vector form of representation of expenses of movement for the
Internet values.

The movement of the Internet values takes place within economic relations. Each of them, as I have already mentioned above, has own
nature of origin—special components.

If we arrange the expenses of economic relations received on a field of
movement of the Internet values on coordinates «X», «Y» and
«Z», on axis «X» we should set the expenses of «production» of
the Internet values. On axis «Y» we should set the expenses of
«distribution» of an Internet values, on axis «Z»—the expenses of
«exchange» of the Internet values.

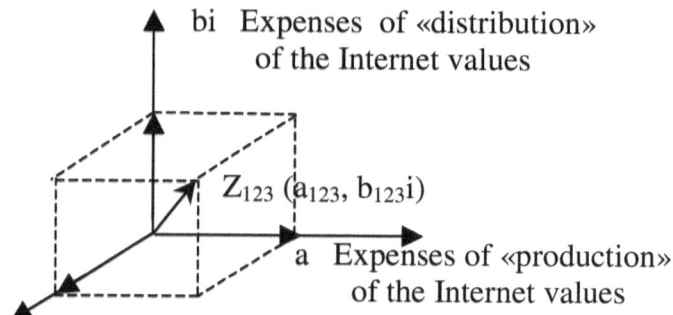

bi Expenses of «distribution»
    of the Internet values

Z_{123} (a_{123}, $b_{123}i$)

a Expenses of «production»
   of the Internet values

Cj Expenses of «exchange» of the Internet values

The total vector under these three economic relations Z_{123} will be written down as follows:

$$Z_{123} = a + bi + cj$$

Where—a—is the expenses of «production» of the Internet
values;

bi—is the expenses of «distribution» of the Internet
values;

cj—is the expenses of «exchange» of the Internet
values.

But we have overlooked «consumption», which, undoubtedly, is part of
general economic relations.

A chain of four economic expenses will be written down as a complex
number—quaternion:

$$Z_{1234} = a + bi + cj + pl$$

Where—p—is the expenses of «consumption» of the Internet
values;

l—is an imaginary unit.

3) The vector form of representation of the expenses for the <u>Internet
services</u>

A movement of the Internet services occurs on all «chain» of economic
relations.

Specificity of this movement is that phases—«production», «distribution», «exchange» and «consumption»—occur simultaneously.

If we arrange the expenses of services (non–material) activity on coordinates «X», «Y», and «Z», on an axis «X» we should set the
expenses of «production» of the Internet services. On an axis «Y»
we should set the expenses of «distribution» of the Internet services. On an axis «Z» we should arrange the expenses of
«exchange» of the Internet services:

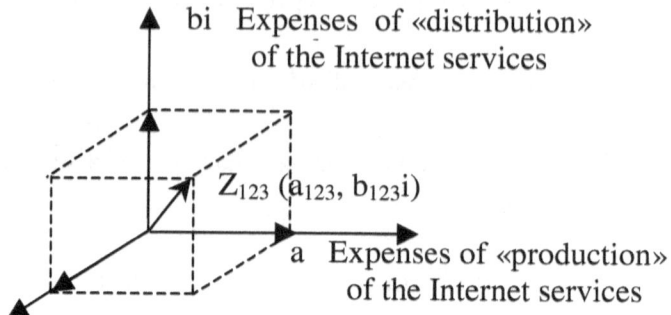

bi Expenses of «distribution»
of the Internet services

Z_{123} (a_{123}, b_{123}i)

a Expenses of «production»
of the Internet services

Cj Expenses of «exchange» of the Internet services

The total vector under these three economic relations will be written down as quaternion.

$$Z_{123} = a + bi + cj$$

Where—a—is the expenses of «production» of the Internet services;

bi—is the expenses of «distribution» of the Internet services;

cj—is the expenses of «exchange» of the Internet services.

Imaginary units—i, j—reflect different (heterogeneous) nature of economic relations.

The chain of economic expenses received in the expenses of movement of the Internet services taking into account the expenses of «consumption» will be written down as a complex number—quaternion:

$$Z_{1234} = a + bi + cj + pl$$

Where—p—is the expenses of «consumption» of the Internet
services;

1—is an imaginary unit.

The Vector Z_{1234} takes different positions in the economic sphere
depending on what economic expenses will take place under each
economic relation.

B) BY SECOND CRITERIA

At a first estimation we see that the material criterion enables the classification of expenses but it is not enough. Here we should use:

– past labor expenses on material and non–material values;

– direct labor expenses on material values and non–material services.

I) The logic structure of values:

Thesis   Material values

Antithesis Non-material values (services)

Synthesis   Aggregate (complex) product

II) The logic structure of expenses:

Thesis   Past labor

Antithesis Direct labor

Synthesis   Aggregate (complex) labor

III) The logic structure of a complex number:

Thesis   Real number—a

Antithesis Imaginary number—bi

Synthesis   Aggregate (complex) number—$Z = a + bi$

These two criteria allow the classification of expenses of Internet values in the context of each economic relation:

Thesis   Past labor expenses—real numbers—a
Antithesis Direct labor expenses—imaginary numbers—bi
Synthesis   Aggregate labor expenses—complex numbers—
$$Z = a + bi$$

Logic of an aggregate product construction, logic of construction of expenses in the context of each economic relation and logic of a complex number are on the same horizontal of consideration. These structures have lined up in one row.

It would be wrong to say that it has happened accidentally. Abstract mathematical truths have concurred with economic logic without rough interface, without a method of analogies etc.

If we connect the first and the third structures, we shall get the following:

Thesis   Material values—real number—a
Antithesis Non–material values (services)—imaginary number—bi
Synthesis   Aggregate (complex) product—aggregate (complex) number—$Z = a + bi$

If we connect the second and the third structures, we will get the following:

Thesis   Past labor—real number—a
Antithesis Direct labor—imaginary number—bi
Synthesis   Aggregate (complex) labor—aggregate (complex) number—$Z = a + bi$

Utilization of complex numbers in economic theory enables us to comprehend that without them we limit ourselves to the truncated variant of consideration not only of problems of expenses, but also of results.

A. Internet values
Expenses connected to the economic relations of «distribution» of Internet values.

Thesis   Past labor expenses—real numbers—a
Antithesis   Direct labor expenses—imaginary numbers—bi
Synthesis   Aggregate labor expenses—complex numbers—
        $Z = a + bi$

Expenses connected to the economic relations of «exchange» of Internet values:

Thesis   Past labor expenses—real numbers—a
Antithesis   Direct labor results—imaginary numbers—bi
Synthesis   Aggregate labor results—complex numbers—
        $Z = a + bi$

Expenses connected to the economic relations of «consumption» of Internet values:

Thesis   Past labor results—real numbers—a
Antithesis   Direct labor expenses—imaginary numbers—bi
Synthesis   Aggregate labor results—complex numbers—
        $Z = a + bi$

B. Internet services
Expenses connected to the economic relations of «distribution» of Internet services:

Thesis   Past labor results—real numbers—a
Antithesis   Direct labor results—imaginary numbers—bi
Synthesis   Aggregate labor results—complex numbers—
        $Z = a + bi$

Expenses connected to the economic relations of «exchange» of
Internet services:

Thesis   Past labor results—real numbers—a
Antithesis Direct labor results—imaginary numbers—bi
Synthesis Aggregate labor results—complex numbers—
        $Z = a + bi$

Expenses connected to the economic relations of «consumption» of
Internet services:

Thesis   Past labor results—real numbers—a
Antithesis Direct labor results—imaginary numbers—bi
Synthesis Aggregate labor results—complex numbers—
        $Z = a + bi$

3. UTILIZATION OF COMPLEX NUMBERS (QUATERNIONS) IN ECONOMIC CALCULATIONS OF EXPENSES CONNECTED TO THE MOVEMENT OF THE INTERNET PRODUCT

A) COMPLEX EXPENSES IN «PRODUCTION» RELATIONS

First it would be necessary to stress that the nature of origin of Internet
values and services is economical: computer and software are created with the input of collective labor estimated at many billions
of labor hours spent on their production.

The same can be said about Internet services (non-material values).
Creation of the existing amount of services is possible with the
investment of hundreds of billions of dollars in this part of the
Internet over a number of years.

Production of Internet values and Internet services takes particular
place in the general system of economic relations (see scheme):

Production	Distribution	Exchange	Consumption
Solitary «production» of Internet values ↓	→ Solitary «distribution» of Internet values ↓	→ Solitary «exchange» of Internet values ↓	→ Solitary «consumption» of Internet values ↓
Expenses within these economic relations	→ Expenses within these economic relations	→ Expenses within these economic relations	→ Expenses within these economic relations
Solitary «production» of Internet services ↓	→ Solitary «distribution» of Internet services ↓	→ Solitary «exchange» of Internet services ↓	→ Solitary «consumption» of Internet services ↓
Expenses within these economic relations	→ Expenses within these economic relations	→ Expenses within these economic relations	→ Expenses within these economic relations
Solitary «production» of Internet products ↓	→ Solitary «distribution» of Internet products ↓	→ Solitary «exchange» of Internet products ↓	→ Solitary «consumption» of Internet products ↓
Expenses within these economic relations	→ Expenses within these economic relations	→ Expenses within these economic relations	→ Expenses within these economic relations

Hence, Internet values differ from Internet services by their nature of origin:

1) Internet values—material nature of origin;
2) Internet services—non-material nature of origin.

These circumstances allow the use of complex numbers in calculating the «expenses». If we set the production expenses of Internet values on the axis of real numbers—X—and production expenses of Internet services on the Y-axis, the vector of expenses of the Internet sphere can be given as a complex number.[10]
The above can be written graphically:

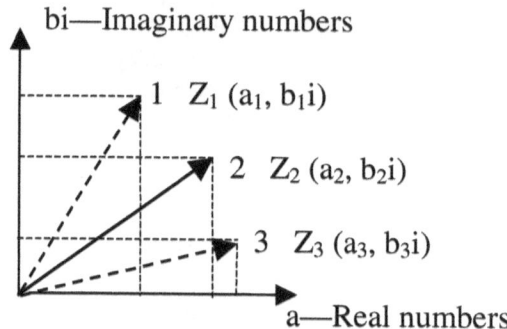

Expenses in the production of Internet values

Z—coordinates of expenses of Internet production while creating Internet values (real numbers) and Internet services (imaginary numbers)

In the figure № we see three possible variants of Internet sphere expenses:

Location of Vector Z_1 shows that in the total expenses of the Internet sphere, the expenses, which are linked with the creation of Internet services, prevail.

---

[10]   **Thesis**   Production expenses of Internet values—«a»

        Antithesis   Production expenses of Internet services—«bi»

        Synthesis   Complex expenses of the Internet sphere of creation of the aggregate Internet product—$Z = a + bi$

Location of Vector Z_2 shows that labor expenses for the production of Internet values and services are equal.

Location of Vector Z_3—here labor expenses for the production of Internet values exceed the expenses connected with the production of Internet services.

1) The above approach in calculating the expenses of the Internet sphere, with the use of complex numbers, has some peculiarities. The essence is that we shall consider this problem both from the point of Internet values and Internet services:

CALCULATION OF LABOR EXPENSES IN THE CREATION
OF INTERNET VALUES WITH THE USE OF COMPLEX NUMBERS

Thesis   Past labor expenses during the creation of Internet values (real number)—«a»

Antithesis Direct labor expenses during the creation of Internet values (imaginary number)– «bi»

Synthesis   Complex labor expenses (past and direct) during the creation of Internet values (complex number)— $Z = a + bi$

The above can be written graphically:

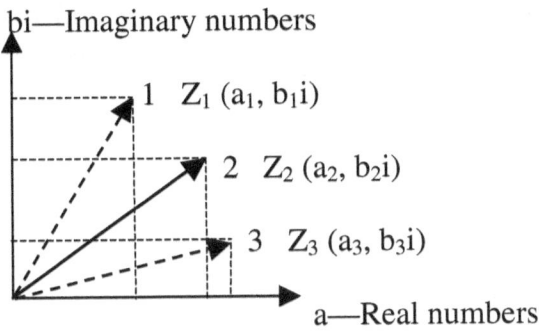

bi—Imaginary numbers

1 $Z_1 (a_1, b_1 i)$

2 $Z_2 (a_2, b_2 i)$

3 $Z_3 (a_3, b_3 i)$

a—Real numbers

Where a—past labor expenses during the creation of Internet values;

bi—direct labor expenses during the creation of Internet values;

$Z(a + bi)$—aggregate labor expenses during the creation of Internet values.

Vector Z takes the first position if direct labor expenses are higher than past labor expenses necessary for the creation of Internet values.

If past labor expenses prevail in the aggregate expenses, the coordinates will be in the zone of Vector Z_3.

2) Besides, complex numbers should also be used in the calculation of Internet services expenses.

CALCULATION OF LABOR EXPENSES DURING THE CREATION OF INTERNET SERVICES WITH THE USE OF COMPLEX NUMBERS

Thesis   Past labor expenses connected to creation of Internet values (real number)—«a»

Antithesis   Direct labor expenses during creation of Internet services (imaginary number)—«bi»

Synthesis   Aggregate labor expenses (past and direct) during creation of Internet services (complex number) $Z = a + bi$

The above can be written graphically:

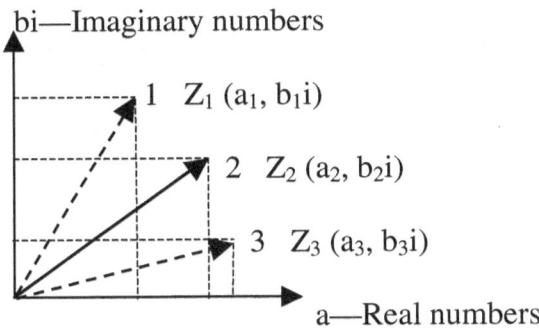

bi—Imaginary numbers

1 Z_1 (a_1, b_1i)

2 Z_2 (a_2, b_2i)

3 Z_3 (a_3, b_3i)

a—Real numbers

Where a—past labor expenses during the distribution of
Internet services (real numbers)

bi—direct labor expenses during the distribution of
Internet services (imaginary numbers)

$Z(a + bi)$—aggregate labor expenses during the distribution of
Internet Services (complex numbers)

Vector Z takes the <u>first position</u> when direct labor expenses are greater
than past labor expenses in the creation of Internet services.

Vector Z takes the <u>third position</u> when expenses of past labor are higher
than direct labor expenses in the creation of Internet services.

In accordance with the fact that the Internet sphere consists of branches
producing Internet values and services, the expenses of this sphere
should be calculated accordingly.

DIALECTICAL STRUCTURE OF EXPENSES CONNECTED TO THE CREATION OF A «COMPLEX INTERNET PRODUCT» ADJUSTED FOR THE OLT RESOURCE

THESIS: «DIALECTICAL STRUCTURE OF LABOR EXPENSES CONNECTED TO THE CREATION OF INTERNET VALUES»

Thesis	Past labor expenses while creating Internet values
Antithesis	Direct labor expenses while creating Internet values
Synthesis	Aggregate labor expenses (past and direct) while creating Internet values

ANTITHESIS: «DIALECTICAL STRUCTURE OF LABOR EXPENSES CONNECTED TO THE CREATION OF INTERNET SERVICES»

Thesis	Past labor expenses while creating Internet services adjusted for the OLT resource
Antithesis	Direct labor expenses while creating Internet services adjusted for the OLT resource
Synthesis	Aggregate labor expenses (past and direct) while creating Internet services adjusted for the OLT resource

SYNTHESIS: «DIALECTICAL STRUCTURE OF EXPENSES CONNECTED TO THE CREATION OF «AGGREGATE INTERNET PRODUCT»

Thesis	Aggregate past labor expenses while creating a «complex Internet product»
Antithesis	Aggregate direct labor expenses while creating a «complex Internet product»
Synthesis	Aggregate labor expenses (past and direct) while creating a «complex Internet product»

The above scheme can be interpreted with the help of complex numbers. But it should be stressed that at this phase of is present of consideration we face the fact that within complex numbers another complex number. In other words, a «complex number» within a «complex number». Let us discuss the problem in detail.

CALCULATION OF COMPLEX EXPENSES IN THE PROCESS OF «PRODUCTION» OF AN INTERNET PRODUCT

LINE A) THESIS   CALCULATION OF LABOR EXPENSES IN THE CREATION OF INTERNET VALUES WITH THE USE OF COMPLEX NUMBERS (REAL NUMBERS)

1st line—Thesis—estimation № 1
Past labor expenses while creating Internet values

2nd line—Antithesis—estimation № 2
Direct labor expenses while creating Internet values

3rd line—Synthesis—estimation № 3
Complex labor expenses while creating Internet values (a complex number in a complex number)—quaternion

LINE B) ANTITHESIS   CALCULATION OF LABOR EXPENSES IN CREATING INTERNET SERVICES WITH THE USE OF COMPLEX NUMBERS (IMAGINARY NUMBERS)

4st line—Thesis—estimation № 4
Past labor expenses while creating Internet services

5nd line—Antithesis—estimation № 5
Direct labor expenses while creating Internet services

6rd line—Synthesis—estimation № 6
   Complex labor expenses while creating Internet services (a
   complex number in a complex number)—quaternion

**LINE C) SYNTHESIS   CALCULATION OF LABOR
EXPENSES IN CREATING A COMPLEX INTERNET PRODUCT
WITH THE USE OF COMPLEX NUMBERS (COMPLEX
NUMBERS)**

7th line—Thesis— estimation № 7
   Past labor expenses while creating Internet products

8th line—Antithesis—estimation № 8
   Direct labor expenses while creating Internet products

9th line—Synthesis—estimation № 9
   Complex labor expenses (past and direct) while creating
   Internet products (a complex number in a complex
   number)—quaternion

The author examines these logical problems to determine where and
   which number is a real number. Where and which number is represented as an imaginary number. Where and which value is represented as a compound–complex number.
The above calculations of expenses can be written down in a form of
   complex numbers (quaternions).

**4. UTILIZATION OF COMPLEX NUMBERS IN ECONOMIC CAL-
CULATIONS OF EXPENSES CONNECTED TO THE MOVE-
MENT OF THE INTERNET PRODUCT WITHIN RELATIONS
OF «DISTRIBUTION»**

Distribution is an economic relation, which arises between people in the
   process of supplying Internet values and services to consumers.

Distribution of Internet values and Internet services takes particular place in the general system of economic relations (see scheme):

Production	Distribution	Exchange	Consumption
Solitary «production» of Internet values ↓	→ Solitary «distribution» of Internet values ↓	→ Solitary «exchange» of Internet values ↓	→ Solitary «consumption» of Internet values ↓
Expenses within these economic relations	→ Expenses within these economic relations	→ Expenses within these economic relations	→ Expenses within these economic relations
Solitary «production» of Internet services ↓	→ Solitary «distribution» of Internet services ↓	→ Solitary «exchange» of Internet services ↓	→ Solitary «consumption» of Internet services ↓
Expenses within these economic relations	→ Expenses within these economic relations	→ Expenses within these economic relations	→ Expenses within these economic relations
Solitary «production» of Internet products ↓	→ Solitary «distribution» of Internet products ↓	→ Solitary «exchange» of Internet products ↓	→ Solitary «consumption» of Internet products ↓
Expenses within these economic relations	→ Expenses within these economic relations	→ Expenses within these economic relations	→ Expenses within these economic relations

During the calculation of the expenses in the field of distribution of
Internet values and services it is necessary to use complex numbers widely. If we set the expenses connected to the distribution of
Internet values on axis of real numbers—X—and the expenses
connected to the distribution of Internet services—on the Y axis,
the number, which reveals the complex expenses linked to distribution can be written as a complex number:

Thesis	Expenses connected to the distribution of Internet values—«a»
Antithesis	Expenses connected to the distribution of Internet services—«bi»
Synthesis	Complex expenses connected to the distribution of the complex Internet product $Z = a + bi$

The above can be written down graphically.

bi—expenses connected to the distribution of Internet services

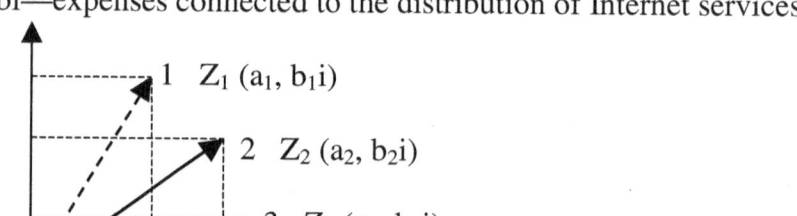

a—expenses connected to the distribution of Internet values

Z—vector of complex expenses connected to the distribution of
Internet values (real numbers) and Internet services (imaginary
numbers).

In figure № we can see three possible variants:

Vector Z_1—the first variant shows that aggregate labor expenses are higher in the total amount of expenses connected to the distribution of the Internet services.

Vector Z_2—in this variant labor expenses for the distribution of Internet values are equal to the expenses for the distribution of Internet services.

Vector Z_3—in this variant of aggregate expenses the greater part goes to the distribution of Internet values.

1) CALCULATION OF LABOR EXPENSES IN THE «DISTRIBUTION» OF INTERNET VALUES (WITH THE USE OF COMPLEX NUMBERS)

The above method of calculating the expenses of the Internet sphere—use of complex numbers—has some peculiarities. I suggest to consider this problem both from the point of Internet values and Internet services:

CALCULATION OF LABOR EXPENSES IN THE «DISTRIBUTION» OF INTERNET VALUES (WITH THE USE OF COMPLEX NUMBERS)

Thesis Past labor expenses connected to distribution of Internet values—(real number)—«a»

Antithesis Direct labor expenses connected to distribution of Internet values—(imaginary number)—«bi»

Synthesis Complex labor expenses (past and direct) connected to distribution of Internet values (complex number)—$Z = a + bi$

The above can be written down graphically:

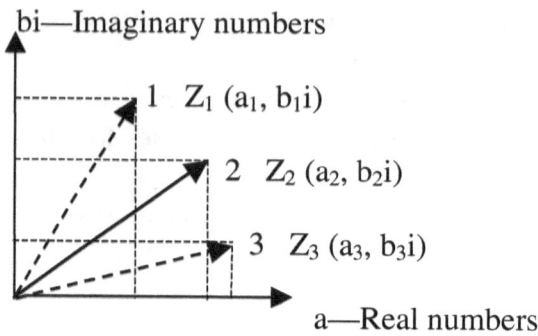

Where a—past labor expenses connected to the distribution of
       Internet values;
       bi—direct labor expenses connected to the distribution of
       Internet values;
Z (a + bi)—aggregate labor expenses connected to the distribu-
       tion of Internet values.

Vector Z_1 takes the <u>first position</u> when direct labor expenses are greater
    than the expenses of past labor connected to the distribution of
    Internet values.
Vector Z_3 takes the <u>third position</u> when past labor expenses are greater
    than the expenses of direct labor connected to the distribution of
    Internet values.

2) Connected to the calculation of the expenses involved in the distribution of Internet services it is necessary to use the following logic:

CALCULATION OF LABOR EXPENSES IN THE «DISTRIBUTION» OF INTERNET SERVICES USING COMPLEX NUMBERS

Thesis   Past labor expenses connected to distribution of Internet services—(real number)—«a»

Antithesis Direct labor expenses connected to distribution of Internet services—(imaginary number)—«bi»

Synthesis   Complex labor expenses (past and direct) connected to the distribution of Internet services—(complex number)—$Z = a + bi$

The above can be written down graphically:

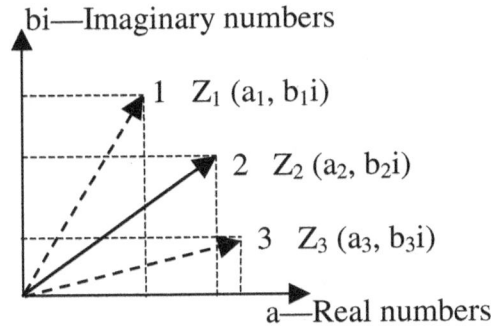

Where a—past labor expenses connected to the distribution of Internet services (real numbers)

   bi—direct labor expenses connected to the distribution of Internet services (imaginary numbers)

$Z (a + bi)$—aggregate labor expenses connected to the distribution of Internet services (complex numbers)

Vector Z_1 takes the <u>first position</u> when direct labor expenses are greater than the expenses of past labor connected to the distribution of Internet services.

Vector Z_3 takes the <u>third position</u> when past labor expenses are greater than the expenses of direct labor connected to the distribution of Internet services.

3) The Internet sphere, as we know, consists of branches producing Internet values and services. Due to this, distribution expenses should be calculated as follows:

DIALECTICAL STRUCTURE OF LABOR EXPENSES CONNECTED TO THE DISTRIBUTION OF A «COMPLEX INTERNET PRODUCT»

THESIS: «DIALECTICAL STRUCTURE OF LABOR EXPENSES CONNECTED TO THE DISTRIBUTION OF INTERNET VALUES»

Thesis	Past labor expenses connected to the distribution of Internet values
Antithesis	Direct labor expenses connected to the distribution of Internet values
Synthesis	Aggregate labor expenses connected to the distribution Internet values

ANTITHESIS: «DIALECTICAL   STRUCTURE   OF   LABOR
EXPENSES CONNECTED TO THE DISTRIBUTION OF
INTERNET SERVICES»

Thesis	Past labor expenses connected to the distribution of Internet services
Antithesis	Direct labor expenses connected to the distribution of Internet services
Synthesis	Aggregate labor expenses connected to the distribution Internet services

SYNTHESIS: «DIALECTICAL STRUCTURE OF LABOR EXPENSES
CONNECTED TO THE DISTRIBUTION OF A «COMPLEX
INTERNET PRODUCT» (WITH THE OLT RESOURCE)»

Thesis	Aggregate past labor expenses connected to the distribution of «complex Internet product»
Antithesis	Aggregate direct labor expenses connected to the distribution of «complex Internet product»
Synthesis	Aggregate labor expenses connected to the distribution of «complex Internet product»

This scheme can be interpreted with the help of complex numbers.
But here we face certain problems concerning the fact that a «complex
number» within a «complex number» is used.

CALCULATION OF EXPENSES CONNECTED TO THE DISTRIBUTION OF INTERNET PRODUCT WITH THE USE COMPLEX NUMBERS

1) THESIS   CALCULATION OF COMPLEX LABOR EXPENSES CONNECTED TO THE «DISTRIBUTION» OF A COMPLEX INTERNET VALUES (WITH THE OLT RESOURCE)

1st line—Thesis—estimation № 1
Past labor expenses connected to the distribution of Internet values

2nd line—Antithesis—estimation № 2
Direct labor expenses connected to the distribution of Internet values

3nd line—Synthesis—estimation № 3
Complex labor expenses connected to the distribution of Internet values (a complex number in a complex number)—quaternion

2) ANTITHESIS CALCULATION OF COMPLEX LABOR EXPENSES CONNECTED TO THE «DISTRIBUTION» OF A COMPLEX INTERNET SERVICES (WITH THE OLT RESOURCE)

4th line—Thesis—estimation № 4
Past labor expenses connected to the distribution of Internet services

5th line—Antithesis—estimation № 5
Direct labor expenses connected to the distribution of Internet services

6th line—Synthesis—estimation № 6
Complex labor expenses connected to the distribution of Internet services (a complex number in a complex number)—quaternion

3) SYNTHESIS CALCULATION OF COMPLEX LABOR EXPENSES CONNECTED TO THE «DISTRIBUTION» OF A COMPLEX INTERNET PRODUCTS (WITH THE OLT RESOURCE)

7th line—Thesis—estimation № 7
Past labor expenses connected to the distribution of Internet products

8th line—Antithesis—estimation № 8
Direct labor expenses connected to the distribution of Internet products

9th line—Synthesis—estimation № 9
Aggregate labor expenses connected to the distribution of Internet products (a complex number in a complex number)—quaternion

The necessity of considering these logical schemes is stipulated by what we have to determine:

Where and which number is real?

Where and which number is an imaginary number?

Where and which value is a complex number?

5. UTILIZATION OF COMPLEX NUMBERS IN ECONOMIC CALCULATIONS OF EXPENSES CONNECTED TO THE MOVEMENT OF THE INTERNET PRODUCT WITHIN RELATIONS OF «EXCHANGE»

Exchange is an economic relation. It is based on the social division of labor. In the development of a social division of labor an exchange has turned into a permanent form of connection between individual commodity producers.

Exchange of Internet values and Internet services takes particular place in the general system of economic relations (see scheme):

Production	Distribution	Exchange	Consumption
Solitary «production» of Internet values ↓	→ Solitary «distribution» of Internet values ↓	→ Solitary «exchange» of Internet values ↓	→ Solitary «consumption» of Internet values ↓
Expenses within these economic relations	→ Expenses within these economic relations	→ Expenses within these economic relations	→ Expenses within these economic relations
Solitary «production» of Internet services ↓	→ Solitary «distribution» of Internet services ↓	→ Solitary «exchange» of Internet services ↓	→ Solitary «consumption» of Internet services ↓
Expenses within these economic relations	→ Expenses within these economic relations	→ Expenses within these economic relations	→ Expenses within these economic relations

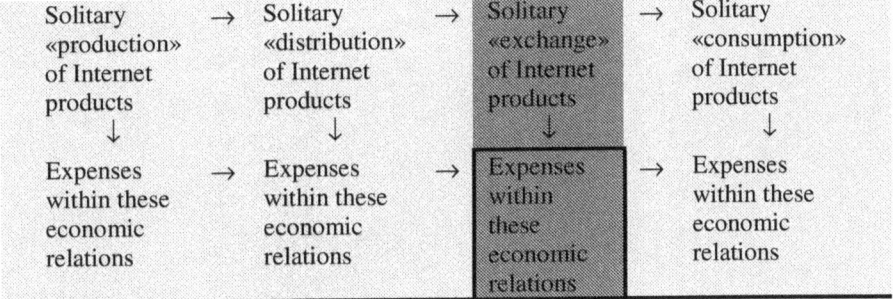

Internet values differ from Internet services by the nature of origin:

1) Internet values—material nature of origin;

2) Internet services—non–material nature of origin.

These circumstances allow us to use complex numbers. If we set exchange expenses of Internet values on an axis of real numbers—X—and on the Y axis the exchange expenses of Internet services, the number which shows the complex expenses can be written down as a complex number.

Thesis   Expenses connected to the exchange of Internet values—«a»

Antithesis   Expenses connected to the exchange of Internet services—«bi»

Synthesis   Complex expenses connected to the exchange of an aggregate complex Internet product—Z = a + bi

The above can be written down graphically:

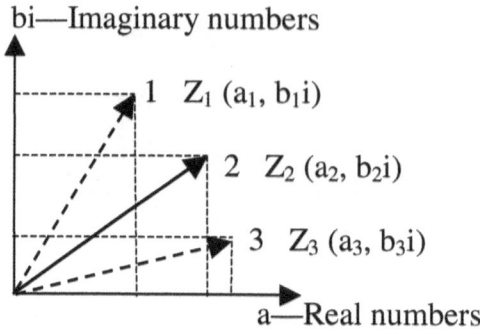

Z—the coordinates of the vector of expenses connected to the exchange of Internet values (real numbers) and Internet services (imaginary numbers).

In diagram № we can see three possible variants of expenses:
  – the first variant shows that expenses connected to exchange exceed the expenses of Internet services.
  – in the second variant the expenses connected to the exchange of Internet values are equal to the expenses of exchange of Internet services.
  – in the third variant labor expenses connected to the exchange of Internet values exceed the expenses of exchange of Internet services.

If the greater part in aggregate expenses goes to the exchange of Internet values, the coordinates will be in the zone of Vector Z_3. If the greater part of total expenses goes to Internet services—vector № 1.

We will concentrate on particular aspects of this problem.
1) The aforementioned method of approach for the calculation of Internet sphere expenses has some peculiarities.

It is important to consider this problem both from the point of Internet values and Internet services:

CALCULATION OF LABOR EXPENSES CONNECTED TO THE EXCHANGE OF INTERNET VALUES

USING COMPLEX NUMBERS

Thesis   Past labor expenses connected to the exchange of Internet values—(real number)—«a»

Antithesis Direct labor expenses connected to the exchange of Internet values—(imaginary number)—«bi»

Synthesis   Complex labor expenses connected to the exchange of Internet values (complex number)—$Z = a + bi$

The above can be written down graphically:

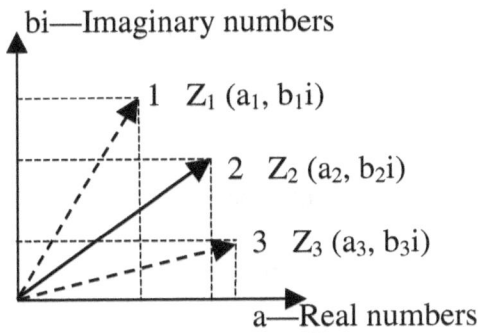

Where a—past labor expenses connected to the exchange of Internet values;

bi—direct labor expenses connected to the exchange of Internet values;

$Z(a + bi)$—aggregate labor expenses connected to the exchange of Internet values.

Vector Z takes the third position if past labor expenses are higher than direct labor expenses connected to the exchange of Internet values.

2) Besides, complex numbers should also be used when calculating the expenses of Internet services.

CALCULATION OF LABOR EXPENSES CONNECTED TO THE EXCHANGE OF INTERNET SERVICES (WITH THE USE OF COMPLEX NUMBERS)

Thesis	Past labor expenses connected to the exchange of Internet services (real number)
Antithesis	Direct labor expenses connected to the exchange of Internet services (imaginary number)
Synthesis	Aggregate labor expenses connected to the exchange of Internet services (complex number)

The above can be written down graphically:

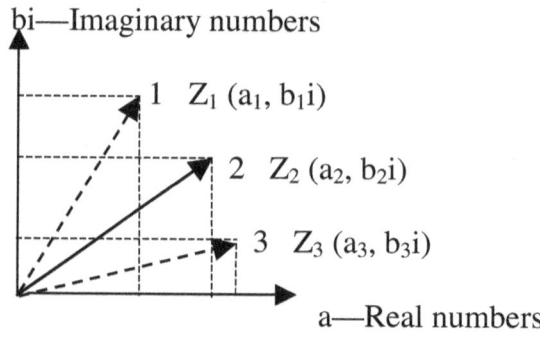

Where a—past labor expenses connected to the exchange of Internet services (real numbers);

bi—direct labor expenses connected to the exchange of Internet services (imaginary numbers);

$Z(a + bi)$—aggregate labor expenses connected to the exchange of Internet services (complex numbers).

Vector Z_1 takes the <u>first position</u> when direct labor expenses are greater than past labor expenses connected to the exchange of Internet services.

Vector Z_3 takes the <u>third position</u> when past labor expenses are greater than direct labor expenses connected to the exchange of Internet services.

The Internet sphere consists of branches producing Internet values and services. The expenses concerning the «exchanges» should be calculated as follows.

DIALECTICAL STRUCTURE OF LABOR EXPENSES CONNECTED TO THE EXCHANGE OF A «COMPLEX INTERNET PRODUCT»

THESIS: «DIALECTICAL STRUCTURE OF LABOR EXPENSES CONNECTED TO THE EXCHANGE OF INTERNET VALUES»

Thesis	Past labor expenses connected to the exchange of Internet values
Antithesis	Direct labor expenses connected to the exchange of Internet values
Synthesis	Aggregate labor expenses connected to the exchange Internet values

ANTITHESIS: «DIALECTICAL STRUCTURE OF LABOR EXPENSES CONNECTED TO THE EXCHANGE OF INTERNET SERVICES»

Thesis   Past labor expenses connected to the exchange of Internet services

Antithesis   Direct labor expenses connected to the exchange of Internet services

Synthesis   Aggregate labor expenses connected to the exchange Internet services

SYNTHESIS: «DIALECTICAL STRUCTURE OF LABOR EXPENSES CONNECTED TO THE EXCHANGE OF A «COMPLEX INTERNET PRODUCT» (WITH THE OLT RESOURCE)»

Thesis   Aggregate past labor expenses connected to the exchange of «complex Internet product»

Antithesis   Aggregate direct labor expenses connected to the exchange of «complex Internet product»

Synthesis   Aggregate labor expenses connected to the exchange of «complex Internet product»

The above scheme can be interpreted with the help of complex numbers, which mathematicians call quaternions. Let us consider this problem in detail:

CALCULATION OF COMPLEX EXPENSES CONNECTED TO THE PROCESS OF «EXCHANGE» OF AN INTERNET PRODUCT (WITH THE OLT RESOURCE)

1) THESIS   CALCULATION OF COMPLEX LABOR EXPENSES CONNECTED TO THE «EXCHANGE» OF A COMPLEX INTERNET VALUES (WITH THE OLT RESOURCE)

1st line—Thesis—estimation № 1
> Past labor expenses connected to the exchange of Internet values

2nd line—Antithesis—estimation № 2
> Direct labor expenses connected to the exchange of Internet values

3nd line—Synthesis—estimation № 3
> Complex labor expenses connected to the exchange of Internet values (a complex number in a complex number)—quaternion

2) ANTITHESIS CALCULATION OF COMPLEX LABOR EXPENSES CONNECTED TO THE «EXCHANGE» OF A COMPLEX INTERNET SERVICES (WITH THE OLT RESOURCE)

4th line—Thesis—estimation № 4
> Past labor expenses connected to the exchange of Internet services

5th line—Antithesis—estimation № 5
> Direct labor expenses connected to the exchange of Internet services

6th line—Synthesis—estimation № 6

Complex labor expenses connected to the exchange of Internet services (a complex number in a complex number)—quaternion

3) SYNTHESIS   CALCULATION OF COMPLEX LABOR EXPENSES CONNECTED TO THE «EXCHANGE» OF A COMPLEX INTERNET   PRODUCTS (WITH THE OLT RESOURCE)

7th line—Thesis—estimation № 7

Past labor expenses connected to the exchange of Internet products

8th line—Antithesis—estimation № 8

Direct labor expenses connected to the exchange of Internet products

9th line—Synthesis—estimation № 9

Aggregate labor expenses connected to the exchange of Internet products (a complex number in a complex number)—quaternion

6. UTILIZATION OF COMPLEX NUMBERS IN ECONOMIC CALCULATIONS OF EXPENSES CONNECTED TO THE MOVEMENT OF THE INTERNET PRODUCT WITHIN RELATIONS OF «CONSUMPTION»

Consumption is the kind of economic relations, which arise between people, at all stages of distributing Internet values, Internet services and aggregate Internet products.

Consumption of Internet values and Internet services takes particular place in the general system of economic relations (see scheme):

Production	Distribution	Exchange	Consumption
Solitary «production» of Internet values $\rightarrow$	Solitary «distribution» of Internet values $\rightarrow$	Solitary «exchange» of Internet values $\rightarrow$	Solitary «consumption» of Internet values
$\downarrow$	$\downarrow$	$\downarrow$	$\downarrow$
Expenses within these economic relations $\rightarrow$	Expenses within these economic relations $\rightarrow$	Expenses within these economic relations $\rightarrow$	Expenses within these economic relations
Solitary «production» of Internet services $\rightarrow$	Solitary «distribution» of Internet services $\rightarrow$	Solitary «exchange» of Internet services $\rightarrow$	Solitary «consumption» of Internet services
$\downarrow$	$\downarrow$	$\downarrow$	$\downarrow$
Expenses within these economic relations $\rightarrow$	Expenses within these economic relations $\rightarrow$	Expenses within these economic relations $\rightarrow$	Expenses within these economic relations
Solitary «production» of Internet products $\rightarrow$	Solitary «distribution» of Internet products $\rightarrow$	Solitary «exchange» of Internet products $\rightarrow$	Solitary «consumption» of Internet products
$\downarrow$	$\downarrow$	$\downarrow$	$\downarrow$
Expenses within these economic relations $\rightarrow$	Expenses within these economic relations $\rightarrow$	Expenses within these economic relations $\rightarrow$	Expenses within these economic relations

Generally it can be shown as follows:

1.DUAL STRUCTURE OF NEEDS
IN THE INTERNET VALUES

Thesis   Production needs in Internet values (real numbers)—a

Antithesis   Non-production (personal) needs in Internet values (imaginary numbers)—bi

Synthesis   Complex needs in Internet values (Z = a + bi)

2. DUAL STRUCTURE OF NEEDS
IN THE INTERNET SERVICES

Thesis   Production needs in Internet services (real numbers)—a

Antithesis   Non-production (personal) needs in Internet services (imaginary numbers)—bi

Synthesis   Complex needs in Internet services (Z = a + bi)

3. DUAL STRUCTURE OF NEEDS
IN THE INTERNET PRODUCT

Thesis   Production needs in Internet product (real numbers)—a

Antithesis   Non-production (personal) needs in Internet product (imaginary numbers)—bi

Synthesis   Complex needs in Internet product (Z = a + bi)

Here it is necessary to use complex numbers. If we set the expenses connected to the «consumption» of Internet values on an axis of real numbers—X—and on the Y axis the expenses connected to the «consumption» of Internet services, the number which shows the complex expenses of the Internet sphere can be written down as a complex number.

Thesis   Expenses connected to the «consumption» of Internet values—«a»

Antithesis Expenses connected to the «consumption» of Internet services—«bi»

Synthesis   Complex expenses connected to the «consumption» of an aggregate complex Internet product of the Internet sphere—$Z = a + bi$

The above can be written down graphically:

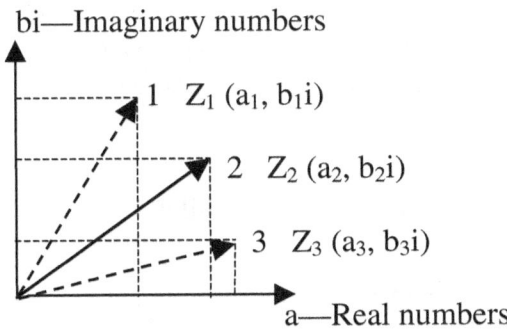

bi—Imaginary numbers

1 $Z_1 (a_1, b_1i)$
2 $Z_2 (a_2, b_2i)$
3 $Z_3 (a_3, b_3i)$

a—Real numbers

Vector Z—shows the expenses within the relations of «consumption» of Internet values (real numbers) and Internet services (imaginary numbers).

If the greater part of aggregate expenses goes to the consumption of Internet values, the coordinates would be in the zone of Vector Z_3. If the greater part of total expenses goes to Internet services the coordinates would be in he zone of Vector Z_1.

1) This method of approaching the calculation of expenses of the Internet sphere—with the use of complex numbers—has some peculiarities. It is important that we consider this problem both in accordance with Internet values and services:

CALCULATION OF LABOR EXPENSES IN THE RELATIONS OF «CONSUMPTION» OF INTERNET VALUES USING COMPLEX NUMBERS

Thesis	Past labor expenses within the relations of «consumption» of Internet values (real number)
Antithesis	Direct labor expenses within the relations of «consumption» of Internet values (imaginary number)
Synthesis	Complex labor expenses (past and direct) within the relations of «consumption» of Internet values (complex number)

The above can be written down graphically:

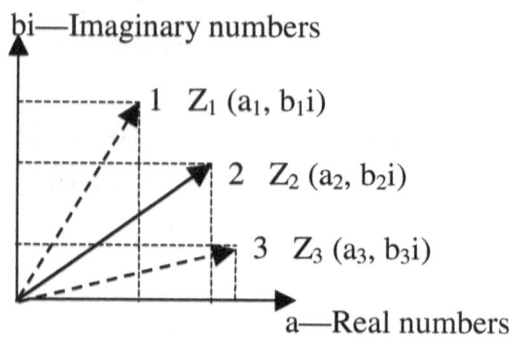

where a—past labor expenses within the relations of «consumption» of Internet values;

bi—direct labor expenses within the relations of «consumption» of Internet values;

$Z(a + bi)$—aggregate labor expenses within the relations of «consumption» of Internet values.

In «consumption» relations Vector Z_1 takes the first position if direct labor expenses are higher than past labor expenses, etc.

2) Besides, complex numbers should be used in calculating the expenses of Internet services within relations of «consumption».

CALCULATION OF LABOR EXPENSES IN THE RELATIONS OF «CONSUMPTION» OF INTERNET VALUES USING COMPLEX NUMBERS

Thesis Past labor expenses within the relations of «consumption» of Internet services (real number)

Antithesis Direct labor expenses within the relations of «consumption» of Internet services (imaginary number)

Synthesis Complex labor expenses (past and direct) within the relations of «consumption» of Internet services (complex number)

The above can be written down graphically:

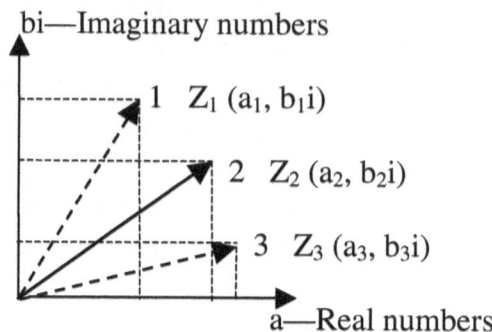

where a—past labor expenses within the relations of «consumption» of Internet services;

bi—direct labor expenses within the relations of «consumption» of Internet services;

$Z(a + bi)$—aggregate labor expenses within the relations of «consumption» of Internet services.

Vector Z takes the <u>first position</u> when direct labor expenses are greater than past labor expenses within relations of «consumption» of Internet services.

Vector Z takes the <u>third position</u> when past labor expenses are greater than direct labor expenses within relations of «consumption» of Internet services.

If we take in consideration that the Internet sphere consists of branches producing Internet values and services, the expenses of the sphere should also be calculated accordingly.

DIALECTICAL STRUCTURE OF LABOR EXPENSES CONNECTED TO THE CONSUMPTION OF A «COMPLEX INTERNET PRODUCT»

THESIS: «DIALECTICAL STRUCTURE OF LABOR EXPENSES CONNECTED TO THE CONSUMPTION OF INTERNET VALUES»

Thesis	Past labor expenses connected to the consumption of Internet values
Antithesis	Direct labor expenses connected to the consumption of Internet values
Synthesis	Aggregate labor expenses connected to the consumption Internet values

ANTITHESIS: «DIALECTICAL STRUCTURE OF LABOR EXPENSES CONNECTED TO THE CONSUMPTION OF INTERNET SERVICES»

Thesis	Past labor expenses connected to the consumption of Internet services
Antithesis	Direct labor expenses connected to the consumption of Internet services
Synthesis	Aggregate labor expenses connected to the consumption Internet services

SYNTHESIS: «DIALECTICAL STRUCTURE OF LABOR EXPENSES CONNECTED TO THE CONSUMPTION OF A «COMPLEX INTERNET PRODUCT» (WITH THE OLT RESOURCE)»

Thesis	Aggregate past labor expenses connected to the consumption of «complex Internet product»
Antithesis	Aggregate direct labor expenses connected to the consumption of «complex Internet product»
Synthesis	Aggregate labor expenses connected to the consumption of «complex Internet product»

The scheme can be interpreted with the help of complex numbers.

CALCULATION OF COMPLEX EXPENSES CONNECTED TO THE PROCESS OF «CONSUMPTION» OF AN INTERNET PRODUCT (WITH THE OLT RESOURCE)

1) THESIS   CALCULATION OF COMPLEX LABOR EXPENSES CONNECTED TO THE «CONSUMPTION» OF A COMPLEX INTERNET VALUES (WITH THE OLT RESOURCE)

1st line—Thesis—estimation № 1
>   Past labor expenses connected to the consumption of Internet values

2nd line—Antithesis—estimation № 2
>   Direct labor expenses connected to the consumption of Internet values

3nd line—Synthesis—estimation № 3
>   Complex labor expenses connected to the consumption of Internet values (a complex number in a complex number)—quaternion

2) ANTITHESIS CALCULATION OF COMPLEX LABOR EXPENSES CONNECTED TO THE «CONSUMPTION» OF A COMPLEX INTERNET SERVICES (WITH THE OLT RESOURCE)

4th line—Thesis—estimation № 4
>   Past labor expenses connected to the consumption of Internet services

5th line—Antithesis—estimation № 5
>
> Direct labor expenses connected to the consumption of
> Internet services

6th line—Synthesis—estimation № 6
>
> Complex labor expenses connected to the consumption of
> Internet services (a complex number in a complex
> number)—quaternion

3) SYNTHESIS   CALCULATION OF COMPLEX LABOR EXPENSES CONNECTED TO THE «CONSUMPTION» OF A COMPLEX INTERNET PRODUCTS (WITH THE OLT RESOURCE)

7th line —Thesis—estimation № 7
>
> Past labor expenses connected to the consumption of
> Internet products

8th line—Antithesis—estimation № 8
>
> Direct labor expenses connected to the consumption of
> Internet products

9th line—Synthesis—estimation № 9
>
> Aggregate labor expenses connected to the consumption of
> Internet products (a complex number in a complex
> number)—quaternion

CALCULATION OF COMPLEX EXPENSES OF THE INTERNET SPHERE CONNECTED TO THE CONSUMPTION PROCESS OF AN INTERNET PRODUCT (WITH THE OLT RESOURCE)

Line A   Thesis (real number) Complex labor expenses connected to the consumption of Internet values.

CALCULATION OF EXPENSES OF THE CONSUMPTION OF INTERNET VALUES

1st line   Thesis—estimation № 1
            Past labor expenses connected to the consumption of
            Internet values (a real number)

2nd line   Antithesis—estimation № 2
            Direct labor expenses connected to the consumption
            of Internet values (imaginary number)

3nd line   Synthesis—estimation № 3
            Aggregate labor expenses (past and direct) connected
            to the consumption of Internet values (compound
            complex number)—quaternion

Line B   Thesis (real number) Complex labor expenses connected to the consumption of Internet services

CALCULATION OF EXPENSES CONNECTED TO THE CONSUMPTION OF INTERNET SERVICES (WITH THE OLT RESOURCE)

4th line   Thesis—estimation № 4
            Past labor expenses connected to the consumption of
            Internet services (real number)

5th line   Antithesis—estimation № 5
Direct labor expenses connected to the consumption of Internet services (imaginary numbers)

6th line   Synthesis—estimation № 6
Aggregate labor expenses (past and direct) connected to the consumption of Internet services (compound complex number)—quaternion

Line C Thesis (<u>real number</u>) Complex labor expenses connected to the consumption of Internet product

CALCULATION OF EXPENSES CONNECTED TO THE CONSUMPTION OF A COMPLEX INTERNET PRODUCT (WITH THE OLT RESOURCE)

7th line   Thesis—estimation № 7
Past labor expenses connected to the consumption of Internet products (real number)

8th line   Antithesis—estimation № 8
Direct labor expenses connected to the consumption of Internet products (imaginary number)

9th line   Synthesis—estimation № 9
Aggregate labor expenses (past and direct) connected to the exchange of Internet products (a compound complex number)—quaternion

The author considers that these logical problems establish precisely where and which number is real.
Where and which number is an imaginary one.
Where and which value is a complex number.

CHAPTER 6. «REAL» AND «IMAGINARY» RESULTS CONNECTED TO THE MOVEMENT OF THE INTERNET PRODUCT

1. NEGATIVE PECULIARITIES OF THE CALCULATION OF ACTIVITY RESULTS

2. PECULIARITIES OF THE ECONOMIC ESTIMATION OF ACTIVITY RESULTS OF THE INTERNET SPHERE

3. UTILIZATION OF QUATERNIONS IN THE ECONOMIC CALCULATION OF THE RESULTS CONNECTED TO THE MOVEMENT OF THE INTERNET PRODUCT

    A. COMPLEX RESULTS CONNECTED TO THE MOVEMENT OF THE INTERNET PRODUCT WITHIN THE RELATIONS OF «PRODUCTION»

B. COMPLEX RESULTS CONNECTED TO THE MOVEMENT OF THE INTERNET PRODUCT WITHIN THE RELATIONS OF «DISTRIBUTION»

C. COMPLEX RESULTS CONNECTED TO THE MOVEMENT OF THE INTERNET PRODUCT WITHIN THE RELATIONS OF «EXCHANGE»

E. COMPLEX RESULTS CONNECTED TO THE MOVEMENT OF THE INTERNET PRODUCT WITHIN THE RELATIONS OF «CONSUMPTION»

1. NEGATIVE PECULIARITIES OF CALCULATION OF ACTIVITY RESULTS

An economic idea for many years has been concentrating its endeavor on investigating the production of material values. It has not had enough time to examine non-material part of economy, which exists parallel to material production.

To form your judgment:

1) In the branches providing intellectual services the following definitions are used as estimate indices—a «televiewer», a «radio listener»; a «visitor» of a museum, library, cinema etc;

2) Spare time of the population in the intellectual sphere is not considered as an economic resource equally with the other resources;

3) In the Internet sphere an index—«visitor»—is the principal definition in the estimation of the results. Here a resource of «On Line Time» (OLT) is not taken into account as an economic component as regards a general stream of resources;

4) In the sphere of public health:

   – part of the population, which has problems with health, is considered as a statistic but not an economic resource;

   – economic evaluation of medical services has not been changing for hundreds of years: the number of visitors, the number of beds;

5) In a sphere of environment economic evaluations have the significant number of logical mistakes;

   a) pollution is estimated without taking into account the factor of time (in the southern seas 1 ton of spilled petroleum is decomposed during 18–24 months), in the northern seas during 50 years (600 months);

b) expenses on overcoming consequences of pollution are not included in a structure of production costs of chemical enterprises, transportation services etc;

6) In the military sphere economic estimations of results are deliberately misinterpreted, produced weapons are interpreted as unaccounted part of the production;

7) In army the results of operations are estimated according to the following showings: the number of killed, the number of wounded. This way of estimation has not changed for hundreds of years;

8) Until now the economy of non-material branches has been developing without any proportions;

9) The conception of the market of non-material values (services) is in a zone of hallucinations;

10) It is not clear how the parameters of the non-material market effect the material one;

11) Economic reference points of the reality are misrepresented;

12) Economic predictions are made without taking into account a significant part of the involved resources. For the same reasons the beginning of crisis processes is defined with delay;

13) Situation in the services part of economy is indefinite. We live in the world of illusions—here there are many times more questions than answers;

14) Analysis of literature proves that in the relatively autonomous spheres of social production—intellectual, medical, military—there is a substitution of categories: «expenses» get an economic status of «results». This makes it possible to represent the increasing expenses as the increasing results. The significant amount of branches, especially the budgetary financing ones, work in a mode: the worse, the better. The expenprinciple of expenses firmly «settled down» in these spheres of economy.

If we put together the above mentioned facts we will see that a conception of non-material results of activity of a significant part of branches of social production is in a zone of illusions. We find ourselves in a kind of a big circus where they manipulate with numbers—«expenses» are represented as «results», on the one hand, and «results» are represented as «expenses» on the other.

It is necessary again and again to consider the problem of estimation of results of activity concerning the relatively autonomous spheres: intellectual, Internet, medical, transport, military etc.

We should begin a consideration of this subject with the notion that for many years in the economic theory of material production specific conception of the method of calculation of a category «result» has taken shape. This method of calculation of results is transferred to branches that stand away from the material production.

The transferring of methods of calculation from one sphere of human activity to another, brings about many mistakes of logical character. The essence of these mistakes is that the results for non-material branches of production of values are calculated in the same way as those in material branches and the idea does not go farther, it stops right there.

On the one hand all rests against economic estimations of utilization of resources in non-material branches, on the other, against absence of criteria of rational utilization of resources.

At present they use contracted criteria omitting some components. Hence, «adequacy» of reflection of economic criteria will be misrepresented. Thus, for example, in the intellectual sphere—a visitor, a cinema goer—discounting the cost component of these resources.

In economic literature a category of «result» is considered in one-dimensional space, using only real numbers. Under «conditions» the category is not revealed properly to meet demands of every day circumstances.

In a category of «result» refraction of many components occurs both positive and negative, and, certainly, here we should use the second and the third spheres of consideration taken from the aspect of material and non-material components of a product, the aspect of economic relations—«production», «distribution», «exchange» and «consumption». A category of result should be revealed in two-, three- and four-dimensional spaces. If a category of result is examined in two spheres it will have two coordinates «X» and «Y». In a three-dimensional sphere it will already have three coordinates—«X», «Y» and «Z».[11]

While considering the first, the second and the third sides of «result» the outlines of a total vector of this category become clear. We quite clearly see components of the result. [12]

So, the first thing we should start from is:

- the «result» should be examined within one economic relation then within another economic relation etc. Our thought avoids making mistakes in this movement.

The movement of the idea is quite natural—from one special aspect of consideration of a category of «result» we pass over to another one etc. [13]

It is <u>unnatural</u> to consider a category of «result» beyond economic relations.

---

[11] It is possible to reveal with the use of complex and supercomplex numbers —quaternions

[12] It is necessary to point out that after using complex numbers you will be reluctant to return to the zone of real numbers since the latter are used in routine relations

[13] The more aspects of this category we examine, the more cognitive the recurrent process will be.

2. PECULIARITIES OF ECONOMIC ESTIMATIONS OF MOVE-MENT OF THE INTERNET RESULTS

Until now a calculation of results has been carried out separately, without connection to economic relations of «production», «distribution», «exchange» and «consumption». I proceed from the point a category of «result» should be considered on the whole way of movement of a product that is in the context of every economic relation:

Production		Distribution		Exchange		Consumption
Solitary «production»	→	Solitary «distribution»	→	Solitary «exchange»	→	Solitary «consumption»
↓		↓		↓		↓
Results of this kind of economic relations	→	Results of this kind of economic relations	→	Results of this kind of economic relations	→	Results of this kind of economic relations

When a production process comes to an end other processes start:
  – a process of «distribution» of the created Internet product;
  – a process of «exchange» of the created Internet product;
  – a process of «consumption» of the created Internet product.

Within each of them there are both expenses and results. In fact, the results as well as expenses within each economic relation can be high and low. Everything depends on the internal arrangement of each of these economic processes of «distribution», «exchange» and «consumption».

Well, it is possible not to divide a category of «result» as regards the kinds of economic relations as well as not to use material and non-material criteria.

Such kind of researches will not have a scientific status but most likely a specific feature from an area of «soft» non-standard lexicon.

1. Calculation of «results» of movement of Internet products can be carried out proceeding from a «narrow» point of view. Its essence is that investigators only consider a service part of the Internet sphere, having overlooked, that there is another group of branches, which create the Internet values—computers and software.

2. Essence of a «wide» point of view: in calculating the results of movement of Internet products is that this sphere is considered an integral economic system consisting of two parts:
   – production of the Internet values;
   – production of the Internet services.

I suggest that the results of movement of an Internet product should be calculated in the context of each economic relation:
   – the results connected to «production» of the Internet values;
   – the results connected to «production» of the Internet services;
   – the results connected to «distribution» of the Internet values;
   – the results connected to «distribution» of the Internet services;
   – the results connected to «exchange» of the Internet values;
   – the results connected to «exchange» of the Internet services;
   – the results connected to «consumption» of the Internet values;
   – the results connected to «consumption» of the Internet services.

In details the above mentioned for the Internet sphere can be written down as follow:

Production	Distribution	Exchange	Consumption
Solitary «production» of Internet values ↓	→ Solitary «distribution» of Internet values ↓	→ Solitary «exchange» of Internet values ↓	→ Solitary «consumption» of Internet values ↓
Results within these economic relations	→ Results within these economic relations	→ Results within these economic relations	→ Results within these economic relations
Solitary «production» of Internet services ↓	→ Solitary «distribution» of Internet services ↓	→ Solitary «exchange» of Internet services ↓	→ Solitary «consumption» of Internet services ↓
Results within these economic relations	→ Results within these economic relations	→ Results within these economic relations	→ Results within these economic relations
Solitary «production» of Internet products ↓	→ Solitary «distribution» of Internet products ↓	→ Solitary «exchange» of Internet products ↓	→ Solitary «consumption» of Internet products ↓
Results within these economic relations	→ Results within these economic relations	→ Results within these economic relations	→ Results within these economic relations

Some of the opponents may object that definition of results within economic relations is not correct for some reasons. In this case, as an exception, I suggest that they consider results of the Internet sphere that will arise on a basis of not economic, but say on a basis of sexual relations.

Substitution of economic relations in the Internet sphere for sexual ones, will undoubtedly give us some results: but what kind of them?

3. UTILIZATION OF QUATERNIONS IN ECONOMIC CALCULATIONS OF RESULTS OF MOVEMENT OF INTERNET PRODUCTS

The aim of the Internet sphere can be considered from several points of view, the principal of which, of course, is economic. But it (economic one) also has a significant number of various aspects:

1. Material and services non-material aspects of consideration;
2. «Expense» and «result» aspects of consideration;
3. Socially useful labor, socially useless labor in the Internet sphere;
4. Utilization of resources involved in the Internet sphere: past, direct and aggregate labor, a resource of «On Line Time» (OLT), included into the process by the Internet services.

There are some other aspects besides the above mentioned to consider the Internet sphere as an economic system. Here, of course, we can build a tree of purposes etc., but it is a separate theme

In this part of the book we will concentrate on consideration of a «result» aspect of movement of an Internet product.

Economic relations, which form between people as regards movement of the Internet values and the Internet services, pass four «inhabitancies»: «production», «distribution», «exchange» and «consumption».

Four «habitats» are heterogeneous as regards their functional destination. Each of the «habitats» of Internet products has its own expenses and own specific results. These relations have their special nature of origin—(as special components).

Here there is every necessary thing to use simple and compound complex numbers:

- different nature of origin of economic relations;
- different nature of origin of Internet products: material and non–material.

C) If we arrange economic relations on coordinates «X», «Y», and «Z», on axis «X» we should set the results of «production» of an Internet product; on axis «Y»—the results of «distribution» of an Complex Internet product; on axis «Z»—the results of «exchange» of an Complex Internet product:

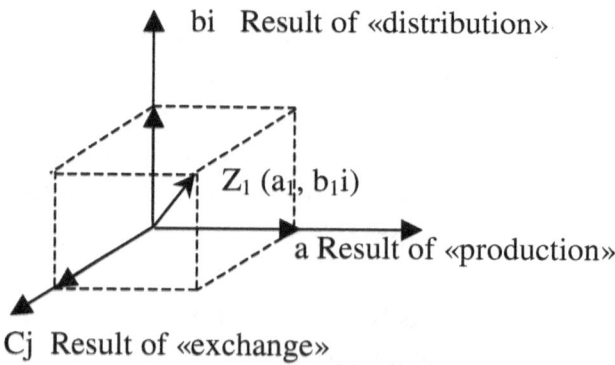

The total vector under these three economic vectors Z_1 will be written down as a compound complex number—quaternion.

$$Z_{123} = a + bi + cj$$

Where—a—a result of «production»;
      bi—a result of «distribution»;
      cj—a result of «exchange».

Imaginary units—i, j—reveal different (heterogeneous) nature of origin of economic relations.

If we proceed from the point that the chain of economic relations consists of:

«production» → «distribution» → «exchange» → «consumption»

the aggregate economic result will be written down as a complex number (quaternion)—the number increased by one more position.

$$Z_{1234} = a + bi + cj + pl$$

Where—p—is a result of «consumption»
      l—is an imaginary unit

Total Vector Z_{1234} will take different positions in the «economic sphere» depending on what kind of results will happen in each economic relation.

A) THE VECTOR FORM OF REPRESENTATION OF RESULTS OF MOVEMENT FOR THE INTERNET VALUES SERVICES

A movement of the Internet values takes place along the entire chain of economic relations.

Specific of this movement is that there phases of «production», «distribution», «exchange» and «consumption» occurs simultaneously.

If we arrange the results of non-material Internet activity on coordinates «X», «Y» and «Z», then we should place production results of Internet values on axis «X». On axis «Y» we should set «distribution» results of Internet values, and on axis «Z» «exchange» results of Internet values should be shown.

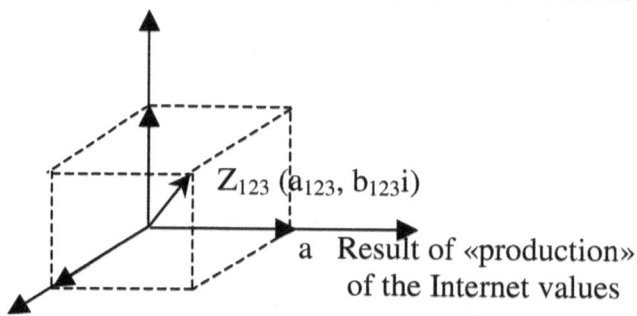

bi Result of «distribution» of the Internet values

$Z_{123} (a_{123}, b_{123}i)$

a Result of «production»
     of the Internet values

Cj Result of «exchange» of the Internet values

The total vector under these three economic relations Z_{123} will be written down as a quaternion:

$$Z_{123} = a + bi + cj$$

where—a—is the result of «production» connected to the movement of the Internet values

bi—is the result of «distribution» connected to the movement of the Internet values

cj—is the result of «exchange» connected to the movement of the Internet values

But we have overlooked «consumption», which, undoubtedly, is part of general economic relations.

A chain of economic results, obtained as a result of Internet value movement adjusted for the results of «consumption» will be written down as a complex number—quaternion:

$$Z_{1234} = a + bi + cj + pl$$

Where—p—is the result of «consumption» of the Internet values;
1—is an imaginary unit.

B) THE VECTOR FORM OF REPRESENTATION OF THE RESULTS FOR THE INTERNET SERVICES

A movement of the Internet services occurs through the sphere of economic relations.

Specificity of this movement is that phases—«production», «distribution», «exchange» and «consumption»—occur simultaneously.

If we arrange the results of services (non-material) activity on coordinates «X», «Y», and «Z», on an axis «X» we should set the results of «production» of the Internet services. On an axis «Y» we should set the results of «distribution» of the Internet services. On an axis «Z» we should arrange the results of «exchange» of the Internet services:

bi   Result of «distribution» of the Internet services

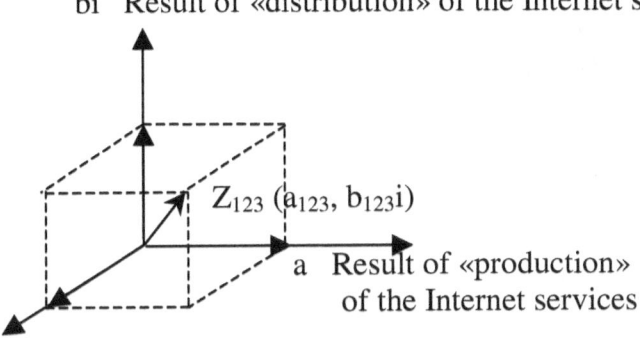

$Z_{123} (a_{123}, b_{123}i)$

a   Result of «production» of the Internet services

Cj   Result of «exchange» of the Internet services

The total vector under these three economic relations will be written down as quaternion.

$$Z_{123} = a + bi + cj$$

Where—a—is the result of «production» connected to the movement of the Internet services;
   bi—is the result of «distribution» connected to the movement of the Internet services;
   Cj—is the result of «exchange» connected to the movement of the Internet services.

Imaginary units—i, j—reflect different (heterogeneous) nature of economic relations.

The chain of economic results received in the result of movement of the Internet services taking into account the results of «consumption» will be written down as a complex number—quaternion:

$$Z_{1234} = a + bi + Cj + pl$$

Where—p—is the result of «consumption» of the Internet services;
   1—is an imaginary unit.

The Vector Z_{1234} takes different positions in the economic sphere depending on what economic results will take place under each economic relation.

A. COMPLEX RESULTS CONNECTED TO THE MOVEMENT OF THE INTERNET PRODUCT WITHIN THE RELATIONS OF «PRODUCTION»

There is substantial economic literature concerning exploitation of manpower in material fields of production. This literature is mainly of Marxist character where an employer is considered an exploiter who «squeezes out vital juices» from workers and peasants. Does this kind of problem exist in the Internet sphere? Who exploits whom and where in the Internet sphere? It is necessary to answer these questions.

Here there is no exploitation of humans by humans, which happened in the past.

Here this problem does not exist.

What kinds of results take place in the Internet sphere of production?

Economic results of Internet sphere activity arise within economic relations, existing inside it. Without economic relations and economic ties between these factors—means of labor, instruments of labor, subjects of labor in the process of production, distribution, exchange and consumption of the Internet values and services, no results, in economic sense of this word, can arise.

This opinion is correct both from the logic and practical points of view. There is no other alternative in the consideration of this problem.

How can we obtain an economic results without economic relations?

While receiving a material Internet results they use past labor, materialized in machines, tools, equipment, automated lines making separate parts of a computers, motherboards etc. Its quota in the results reaches 97%. Here the results are formed by past labor.

While receiving a material Internet result they use direct labor of programmers, who create new technologies of processing information. If we consider the activity of companies, producing database software, maybe we can find some kind of exploitation there, but qualified employees earn above US$ 10,000 monthly. Besides, development of software products is a creative activity of an inventive character.

If we consider the activity of the Internet companies rendering services, here we will find that transfer operations are carried out by technical means with the use of various programs. The role of direct labor is kept at a minimum of 0.000001 %.

A service sector of the Internet brings comfort to people. These services reduce direct labor expenses (as well as past) that occur: while buying food things, tickets; in banking activity, in a sector of services provided by the state etc.

Internet services reduce expenses of spare time and make it more compact, expanding the borders of spare time of population.

In the Internet sphere they master a spare time of population resource. Here we deal with not a direct but implied exploitation of human resources. The more human resources involved in the Internet service, the less the time left for any other kind of activity. In other words the Internet services take away part of a person's freedom.

Generally the logic of the problem can be represented as follows:

1) Exploitation of internal resources (exploitation of past laboring the Internet)

1. Thesis   Exploitation of past labor in the first division of the Internet sphere—«a»

2. Antithesis   Exploitation of past labor in the second division of the Internet sphere—«bi»

3. Synthesis   Aggregate exploitation of past labor in the Internet sphere: $Z = a + bi$

2) Exploitation of internal resources (exploitation of direct labor in the Internet)

1. Thesis   Exploitation of direct labor in the 1st division of the Internet sphere—«a»

2. Antithesis Exploitation of direct labor in the 2nd division of the Internet sphere—«bi»

3. Synthesis Aggregate exploitation of direct labor in the Internet sphere

3) Exploitation of external resources

1. Thesis   Exploitation of human resources by Internet sphere services during working hours—«a»

2. Antithesis Exploitation of human resources by the services of the Internet service sphere during working hours—«bi»

3. Synthesis Aggregate exploitation of human resources during working hours and spare time in the Internet sphere—$Z = a + bi$

A RESULT OF PRODUCTION IN THE INTERNET SPHERE

In the Internet sphere employees enter economic relations between each other by participating in the production of Internet values. They enter economic relations with the society through the results of their Internet labor.

Division of the entire amount of the created Internet products into «material» and «non–material» is a necessary initial moment of classification of the results of this sphere. This allows us to use complex numbers in the part of calculation of the «results».

If we arrange the results of the Internet values production on axis «X» and the results of the Internet services production on axis «Y», the quantity reflecting complex results of the Internet sphere can be reordered as a complex number:

1. Thesis   Results of production of Internet values—«a»
2. Antithesis Results of production of Internet services—«bi»
3. Synthesis   Complex results of the Internet sphere on the creation of an aggregate complex Internet product
$Z = a + bi$

Z—coordinates of the complex result of the Internet production

The above can be shown graphically:

bi Imaginary numbers—Results of production of Internet services

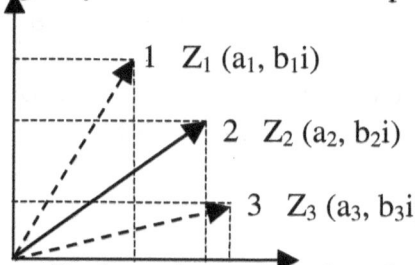

1 $Z_1 (a_1, b_1 i)$

2 $Z_2 (a_2, b_2 i)$

3 $Z_3 (a_3, b_3 i)$

a Real numbers—Results of production of Internet values

In picture № we see three possible variants of the results of the Internet sphere:

1) Vector $Z (a_1, b_1 i)$ shows that in the entire amount of the results of the Internet sphere, the results concerning the Internet services prevail.
2) Vector $Z (a_2, b_2 i)$ shows that the results of production of Internet values and services are equal.

3) In the third variant Z (a_3, b_3i) the results of production of the Internet values prevail over the results connected to the production of the Internet services.

Let us concentrate on the particular aspects of this problem, and in particular.

1) Consider the calculation of the results on Internet values:

STRUCTURE OF THE RESULTS OF INTERNET VALUES PRODUCTION

1. Thesis   Results of past labor while creating Internet values (a real number)

2. Antithesis Results of direct labor while creating Internet values (an imaginary number)

3. Synthesis Complex results of labor (past and direct) while creating Internet values (a complex number)

The above can be shown graphically:

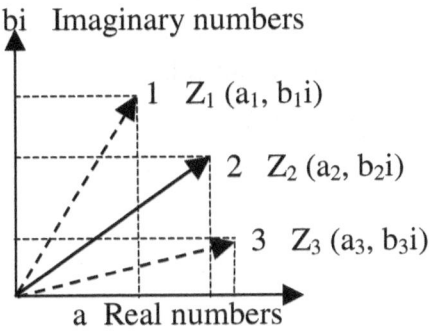

Where a—results of past labor while creating Internet values;
    bi—results of direct labor while creating Internet values;
$Z(a + bi)$—results of aggregate labor while creating Internet values.

Vector Z takes the <u>first position</u> when the results of the production of direct labor are higher than those of past labor while exchanging the Internet services.

Vector Z takes the third position when the results of the production of past labor are higher than those of direct labor during the exchange of Internet services.

In case of equality of the results of the production Vector Z is on a bisector of angle φ—the second position.

STRUCTURE OF RESULTS OF INTERNET SERVICES PRODUCTION

1. Thesis   Results of past labor while creating Internet services, taking into account OLT (real number)

2. Antithesis Results of direct labor while creating Internet services, taking into account OLT (imaginary number)

3. Synthesis Aggregate results of labor while creating Internet services, taking into account OLT (complex number)

The above can be shown graphically:

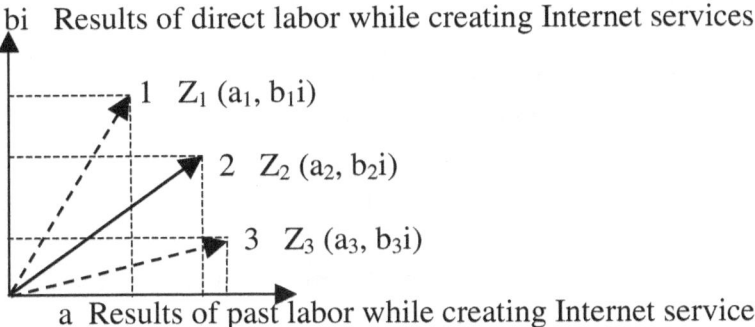

bi   Results of direct labor while creating Internet services

1   $Z_1 (a_1, b_1i)$

2   $Z_2 (a_2, b_2i)$

3   $Z_3 (a_3, b_3i)$

a   Results of past labor while creating Internet services

where—a—results of past labor while creating Internet services
(real numbers)

bi—results of direct labor while creating Internet services
(imaginary numbers)

Z(a +bi)—results of aggregate labor while creating Internet services (complex numbers)

Vector Z takes the <u>first position</u> when the results of direct labor exceed
the results of past labor while creating Internet services.

Vector Z takes the <u>third position</u> when the results of past labor exceed
the results of direct labor while creating Internet services.

If the results within relations of «production» are equal Vector Z is on
the bisector of angle φ.

3) If we consider that the Internet sphere consists of branches producing Internet values and services, the results of the sphere under consideration will be calculated as follows:

COMPLEX STRUCTURE OF RESULTS OF INTERNET PRODUCTION

1. Results of Internet sphere branches during the creation of Internet values.
2. Results of Internet sphere branches during the creation of Internet services, taking into account OLT.
3. Total: Results of Internet sphere = (Results of branches producing Internet values plus the results of branches producing Internet services, taking into account OLT.

The problem of calculation of results within production can be represented in details as follows:

DIALECTICAL STRUCTURE OF RESULTS CONNECTED TO THE PRODUCTION OF «COMPLEX INTERNET PRODUCT» TAKING INTO ACCOUNT OLT RESOURCE

THESIS

DIALECTICAL STRUCTURE OF LABOR RESULTS WHILE CREATING INTERNET VALUES

Thesis   Results of past labor while creating Internet values
Antithesis Results of direct labor while creating Internet values
Synthesis   Results of aggregate labor while creating Internet values

ANTITHESIS

DIALECTICAL STRUCTURE
OF LABOR RESULTS
WHILE CREATING INTERNET SERVICES

Thesis   Results of past labor while creating Internet services
Antithesis Results of direct labor while creating Internet services
Synthesis   Results of aggregate labor while creating Internet services

ANTITHESIS

DIALECTICAL STRUCTURE OF
RESULTS WHILE CREATING
«AGGREGATE INTERNET PRODUCT»

Thesis   Aggregate past labor results while creating an «aggregate Internet product» (taking into account OLT resource)

Antithesis Aggregate direct labor expenses while creating an «aggregate Internet product» (taking into account OLT resource)

Synthesis   Aggregate labor results (indirect and direct) while creating an «aggregate Internet product» (taking into account a OLT resource)

At this stage of considering the peculiarities of complex number use while calculating the results of the Internet sphere, we come across the fact that within a complex number another complex number «is present». Let us consider this problem in detail.

CALCULATION OF COMPLEX RESULTS OF THE INTERNET SPHERE WITHIN «PRODUCTION» RELATIONS

1) Thesis   Complex results of labor while creating Internet values (real numbers)

CALCULATION OF COMPLEX RESULTS OF THE INTERNET
VALUES WITHIN «PRODUCTION» RELATIONS

1st line— Thesis—estimation № 1
   Results of past labor while creating Internet values

2nd line—Antithesis—estimation № 2
   Results of direct labor while creating Internet values

3rd line—Synthesis—estimation № 3
   Aggregate results of labor while creating Internet values
   (complex number in complex number)—quaternion

2) Antithesis   Complex results of labor while creating Internet services (real numbers)

CALCULATION OF COMPLEX RESULTS OF THE INTERNET
SERVICES WITHIN «PRODUCTION» RELATIONS

4st line—Thesis—estimation № 4
   Results of past labor while creating Internet services

5nd line—Antithesis—estimation № 5
   Results of direct labor while creating Internet services

6rd line—Synthesis—estimation № 6
   Aggregate results of labor while creating Internet services
   (complex number in complex number)—quaternion

3) Synthesis　Aggregate results of labor of the Internet sphere while creating an Internet product (complex numbers)

CALCULATION OF COMPLEX RESULTS OF THE INTERNET PRODUCTS WITHIN «PRODUCTION» RELATIONS

7th line—Thesis—estimation № 7
   Results of past labor while creating an Internet product, taking into account OLT resource

8th line—Antithesis—estimation № 8
   Results of direct labor while creating an Internet product, taking into account OLT resource

9th line—Synthesis—estimation № 9
   Aggregate results of labor while creating an Internet product, taking into account OLT resource (complex number in complex number)—quaternion.

B. COMPLEX RESULTS CONNECTED TO THE MOVEMENT OF THE INTERNET PRODUCT WITHIN THE RELATIONS OF «DISTRIBUTION»

Relations of distribution in the Internet sphere are a part of general economic relations existing in society. Getting Internet values and services to a consumer is connected to their distribution and to the results of their distribution.

The results of distribution can be different. Everything depends on what kind of aims, and criteria are put in the basis ofdistribution.

If they use not structurally arranged totality of criteria, the results of distribution will be at a low qualitative level.

On the contrary if they use logic criteria, the result will be appropriate. So, for example, Internet values as any other material values enter the market traditionally. Here the distribution criteria should also be traditional. Internet services enter the market untraditionally. In connection to that the criteria should also be special.

The relation of «distribution» should be considered from two sides: as a category having dual character:

- results of an «internal distribution» in the frames of Internet sphere;
- results of an «external distribution» out of the Internet sphere.

If we add the material and non-material components of distribution to these aspects of consideration, in such a classification of the results of distribution everything finds its proper place.

A) THE RESULTS OF ACTIVITY WITHIN DISTRIBUTIVE ECO-NOMIC RELATIONS

If to consider the distributive relations in the Internet sphere in the light of the material and non-material results of activity, there are peculiarities in the results of movement of the Internet values and services form a producer to a customer. So, for example, in the distribution of Internet values—computers and software—the significant place belongs to the transport component. It improves the economic properties of these values—consumer, cost, and exchange.

In the distribution of Internet services in time and space a transport component is absent but other components are available—communication and so on.

If to examine this problem from the opposite point:
- without classification of the results of internal and external distribution;
- without classification of the results of distribution received on a stream of Internet values and services;
- without classification of the particular results—it will be very difficult to understand the problems of distribution.

In my classification of the results of distribution everything becomes much easier, everything finds its proper place.

In its movement the Internet product breaks up into two components: movement of Internet values and movement of Internet services:

Production	Distribution	Exchange	Consumption
Solitary «production» of Internet values ↓	→ Solitary «distribution» of Internet values ↓	→ Solitary «exchange» of Internet values ↓	→ Solitary «consumption» of Internet values ↓
Results within these economic relations	→ Results within these economic relations	→ Results within these economic relations	→ Results within these economic relations
Solitary «production» of Internet services ↓	→ Solitary «distribution» of Internet services ↓	→ Solitary «exchange» of Internet services ↓	→ Solitary «consumption» of Internet services ↓
Results within these economic relations	→ Results within these economic relations	→ Results within these economic relations	→ Results within these economic relations

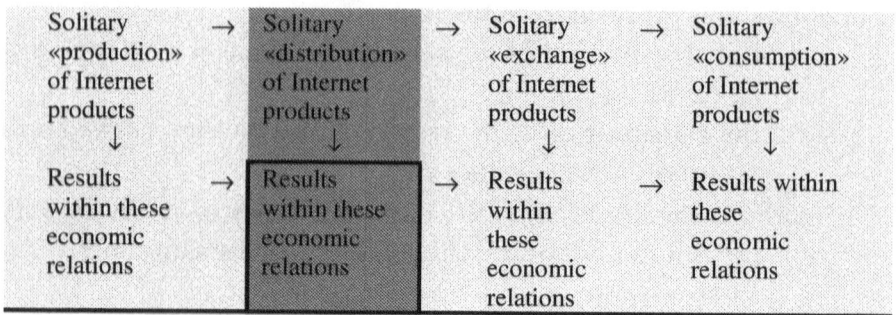

If to show the results, connected to distribution of the Internet values, on the X axis of real numbers, and the results of distribution of the Internet services on the Y axis, the number revealing the complex results out of the Internet sphere connected to the distribution can be written in a form of a complex number.[14]

CALCULATION OF RESULTS OF «DISTRIBUTION»
OUT OF THE INTERNET SPHERE USING COMPLEX NUMBERS

1. Thesis   Results connected to the distribution of Internet values—«a»

2. Antithesis   Results connected to the distribution of Internet services—«bi»

3. Synthesis   Complex results of the Internet sphere connected to the distribution of an aggregate (complex) Internet product $Z = a + bi$

---

[14] In other words within the relations of «distribution» the result can be both positive and negative.

Z—vector of the complex results connected to distribution of Internet values (real numbers) and Internet services (imaginary numbers).

The above can be written graphically:

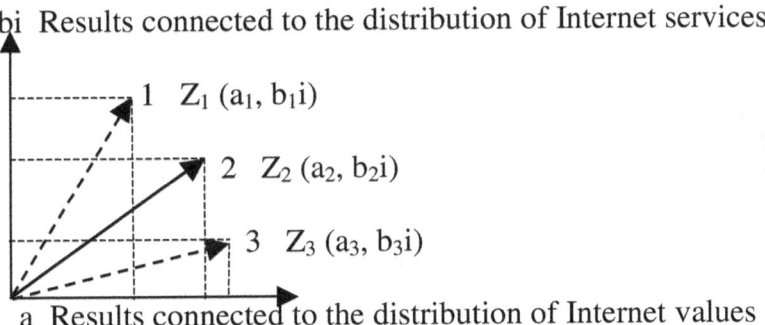

bi Results connected to the distribution of Internet services

1 Z_1 (a_1, b_1i)

2 Z_2 (a_2, b_2i)

3 Z_3 (a_3, b_3i)

a Results connected to the distribution of Internet values

If in the aggregate result of distribution the results during distribution of the values prevail, the coordinates of Vector Z will be a_3, b_3i.

If in the general results the results of the Internet services prevail, Vector Z will take the first position.

In case of equality of the results of distribution of Internet values and services Vector Z takes the second position.

The material and non-material nature of origin of Internet values and services allows us to use complex numbers in the calculation of the «results».

CALCULATION OF THE RESULTS CONNECTED TO THE «DISTRIBUTION» OF INTERNET VALUES USING COMPLEX NUMBERS

1. Thesis   Results of past labor while distributing Internet values (a real number)

2. Antithesis Results of direct labor while distributing Internet values (an imaginary number)

3. Synthesis Complex results of labor while distributing Internet values (a complex number)

The above can be shown graphically:

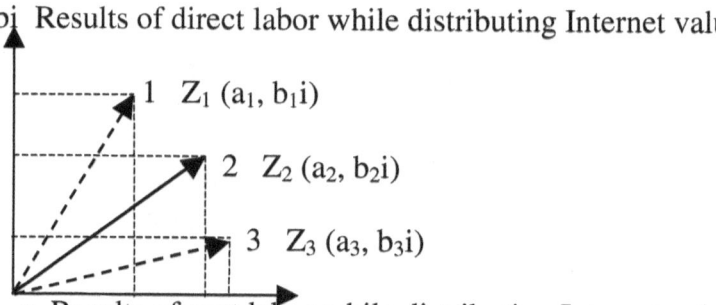

bi Results of direct labor while distributing Internet values

1   Z_1 (a_1, b_1i)

2   Z_2 (a_2, b_2i)

3   Z_3 (a_3, b_3i)

a Results of past labor while distributing Internet values

Where—a—results of past labor while distributing Internet values;

bi—results of direct labor while distributing Internet values;

Z (a +bi)—results of aggregate labor while distributing Internet values.

Vector Z takes the third position if the results of past labor prevail over the results of direct labor. Vector Z takes position № 1 if the results of direct labor prevail over the results of past labor.

In case of equality of the results of distribution of Internet values Vector Z takes the second position.

CALCULATION OF RESULTS CONNECTED TO THE DISTRIBUTION OF THE INTERNET SERVICES USING COMPLEX NUMBERS

1. Thesis   Results of past labor while distributing Internet services, taking into account OLT resource

2. Antithesis Results of direct labor while distributing Internet services, taking into account OLT resource

3. Synthesis   Aggregate results of labor while distributing Internet services, taking into account OLT resource

The above can be shown graphically:

bi—results of direct labor while distributing Internet services

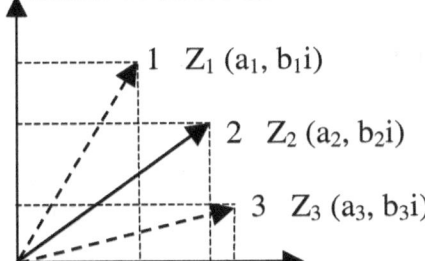

1   Z_1 (a_1, b_1i)

2   Z_2 (a_2, b_2i)

3   Z_3 (a_3, b_3i)

a results of past labor while distributing Internet services

Where—a—results of past labor while distributing Internet services, taking into account OLT resource;

bi—results of direct labor while distributing Internet services, taking into account OLT resource;

Z(a + bi)—results of aggregate labor while distributing Internet services, taking into account OLT resource (complex numbers).

Vector Z takes the <u>first position</u> when direct labor results are higher than that of past labor while distributing Internet services.

Vector Z takes the third position when past labor results are higher that of direct labor while distributing Internet services.

3) Generally view the result within distributive relations will be written down as follows:

1. Results of distribution of Internet values;
2. Results of distribution of Internet services, taking into account OLT resource;
3. Total: Results of distribution of Internet values plus results of branches involved into the distribution of Internet services, taking into account OLT resource.

Lets examine this problem in detail:

DIALECTICAL STRUCTURE OF RESULTS CONNECTED TO «DISTRIBUTION» OF «COMPLEX INTERNET PRODUCT», WITH CONSIDERATION OF OLT RESOURCE

THESIS

DIALECTICAL STRUCTURE OF RESULTS WHILE DISTRIBUTING INTERNET VALUES

Thesis   Results of past labor while distributing Internet values
Antithesis Results of direct labor while distributing Internet values
Synthesis   Results of aggregate labor while distributing the Internet values

ANTITHESIS

DIALECTICAL STRUCTURE
OF THE RESULTS WHILE DISTRIBUTING THE INTERNET
SERVICES

Thesis Past labor results while distributing Internet services taking into account OLT resource

Antithesis Direct labor while results distributing Internet services, taking into account OLT resource

Synthesis Aggregate labor results while distributing Internet services, taking into account OLT resource

SYNTHESIS

DIALECTICAL STRUCTURE
OF RESULTS WHILE DISTRIBUTING AN COMPLEX INTERNET
PRODUCT

Thesis Complex results of past labor while distributing an «aggregate Internet product», taking into account OLT resource

Antithesis Complex results of direct labor while distributing an «aggregate Internet product», taking into account OLT resource

Synthesis Complex results of labor while distributing an «aggregate Internet product», taking into account OLT resource

Let us examine this problem in detail using simple and compound complex numbers—quaternion.

COMPLEX RESULTS CONNECTED TO THE MOVEMENT OF THE INTERNET PRODUCT WITHIN THE RELATIONS OF «DISTRIBUTION»

1) Thesis   Complex results of labor while distributing Internet values (real numbers)

CALCULATION OF COMPLEX RESULTS OF THE INTERNET
VALUES WITHIN «DISTRIBUTION» RELATIONS

1st line—Thesis—estimation № 1
Results of past labor while distributing Internet values

2nd line—Antithesis—estimation № 2
Results of direct labor while distributing Internet values

3rd line—Synthesis—estimation № 3
Aggregate results of labor while distributing Internet values
(complex number in complex number)—quaternion

2) Antithesis Complex results of labor while distributing Internet services (real numbers)

CALCULATION OF COMPLEX RESULTS OF THE INTERNET
SERVICES WITHIN «DISTRIBUTION» RELATIONS

4st line—Thesis—estimation № 4
Results of past labor while distributing Internet services

5nd line—Antithesis—estimation № 5
Results of direct labor while distributing Internet services

6rd line—Synthesis—estimation № 6
Aggregate results of labor while distributing Internet services
(complex number in complex number)—quaternion

3) Synthesis Aggregate results of labor of the Internet sphere while distributing an Internet product (complex numbers)

CALCULATION OF COMPLEX RESULTS OF THE INTERNET PRODUCTS WITHIN «DISTRIBUTION» RELATIONS

7th line—Thesis—estimation № 7
> Results of past labor while distributing an Internet product, taking into account OLT resource

8th line—Antithesis—estimation № 8
> Results of direct labor while distributing an Internet product, taking into account OLT resource

9th line—Synthesis—estimation № 9
> Aggregate results of labor while distributing an Internet product, taking into account OLT resource (complex number in complex number)—quaternion.

C. COMPLEX RESULTS CONNECTED TO THE MOVEMENT OF THE INTERNET PRODUCT WITHIN THE RELATIONS OF «EXCHANGE»

Relations of exchange of Internet values and services provide connection of two hemispheres—between the first and the second divisions of the Internet sphere.

In its movement the Internet product breaks up into two components—
movement of Internet values and movement of Internet services:

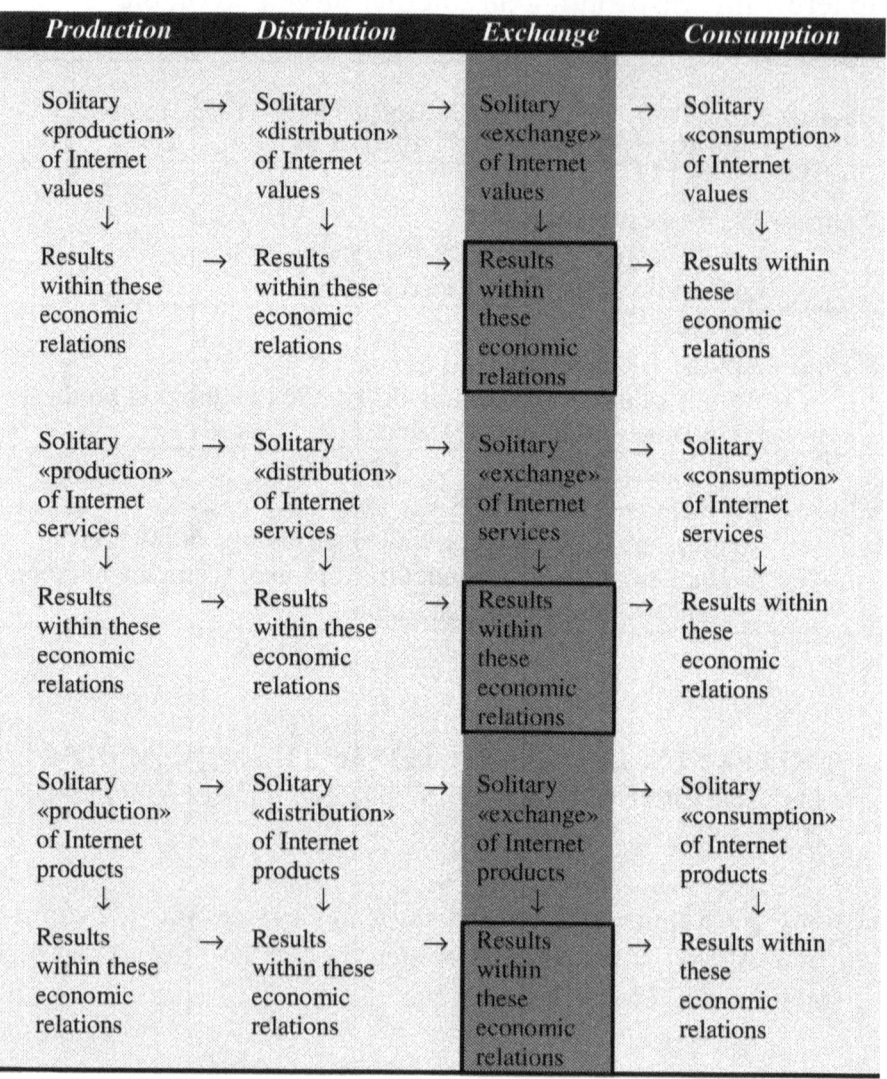

Production	Distribution	Exchange	Consumption
Solitary «production» of Internet values $\downarrow$	$\rightarrow$ Solitary «distribution» of Internet values $\downarrow$	$\rightarrow$ Solitary «exchange» of Internet values $\downarrow$	$\rightarrow$ Solitary «consumption» of Internet values $\downarrow$
Results within these economic relations	$\rightarrow$ Results within these economic relations	$\rightarrow$ Results within these economic relations	$\rightarrow$ Results within these economic relations
Solitary «production» of Internet services $\downarrow$	$\rightarrow$ Solitary «distribution» of Internet services $\downarrow$	$\rightarrow$ Solitary «exchange» of Internet services $\downarrow$	$\rightarrow$ Solitary «consumption» of Internet services $\downarrow$
Results within these economic relations	$\rightarrow$ Results within these economic relations	$\rightarrow$ Results within these economic relations	$\rightarrow$ Results within these economic relations
Solitary «production» of Internet products $\downarrow$	$\rightarrow$ Solitary «distribution» of Internet products $\downarrow$	$\rightarrow$ Solitary «exchange» of Internet products $\downarrow$	$\rightarrow$ Solitary «consumption» of Internet products $\downarrow$
Results within these economic relations	$\rightarrow$ Results within these economic relations	$\rightarrow$ Results within these economic relations	$\rightarrow$ Results within these economic relations

In other words within the relations of an «exchange» the result can be both positive and negative.

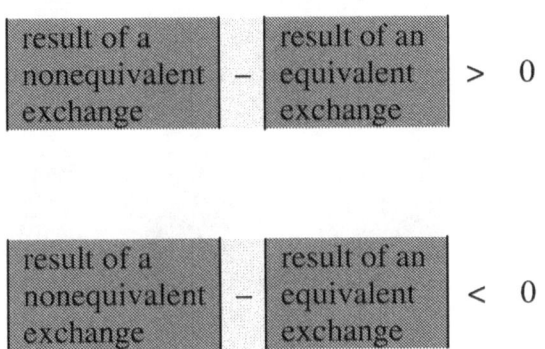

If some part of the involved resources is not taken into account, in the «result» category, the result of the exchange will be the following:

1st variant

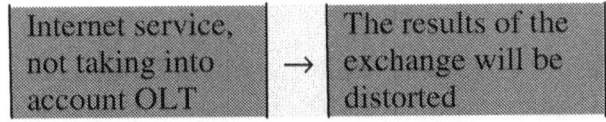

a) in this case on the one side there will be those persons who get extra profits on a field of «resources not taken into account»;
b) on the other side there will be those people who will not get profits for the same reason. These circumstances should worry not only economists and professors, but first of all, ordinary citizens. The population is economically interested in the inclusion of the spare time resource into the cost of the Internet services much more than the Internet companies are.

2nd variant

Relations of exchange have been considered taking into account all economic resources involved in the Internet sphere, including the «spare time of population» resource.

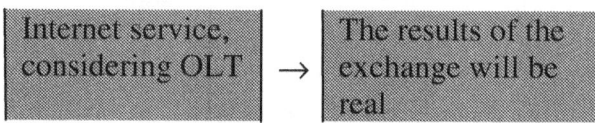

We have already pointed out that the Internet values differ from Internet services by nature of origin. This circumstance allows us to use complex numbers.

To show the results connected to the exchange of Internet values on a real number axis—X—the results connected to the exchange of the Internet services on the Y axis, the number revealing the complex results of the Internet sphere within the exchange relations can be written as follows:

1. Thesis   Results while exchanging Internet values—a
2. Antithesis   Results while exchanging Internet services, taking into account OLT resource—bi
3. Synthesis   Complex results of the Internet sphere while exchanging an aggregate complex Internet product, taking into account OLT resource—Z = a + bi

Z—vector of the complex result while exchanging Internet values (real numbers) and Internet services (imaginary numbers)

The above can be shown graphically:

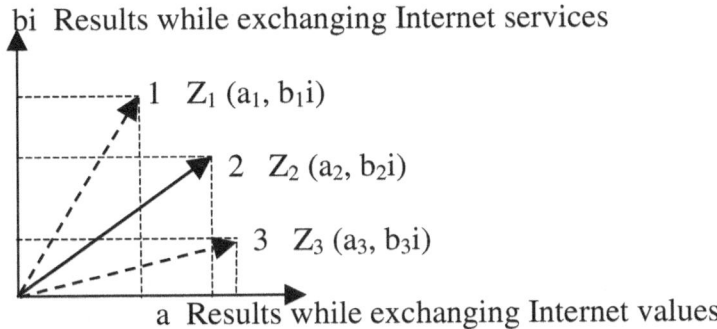

bi Results while exchanging Internet services

1 Z_1 (a_1, b_1i)

2 Z_2 (a_2, b_2i)

3 Z_3 (a_3, b_3i)

a Results while exchanging Internet values

If in the aggregate results of the exchange of an Internet product the results received at the «field» of Internet services prevail, Vector Z takes the first position, and conversely it takes the third position. In case of equality of the results Vector Z takes the second position.

Let us examine the particular aspects of this problem regarding both Internet values and services.

1) Calculation of results of an exchange of Internet values.

CALCULATION OF THE RESULTS OF AN EXCHANGE OF INTERNET VALUES WITH THE USE OF COMPLEX NUMBERS

1. Thesis   Past labor results while exchanging Internet values (real number)

2. Antithesis   Direct labor results while exchanging Internet values (imaginary number)

3. Synthesis   Complex results of labor while exchanging Internet values (complex number)

The above can be shown graphically:

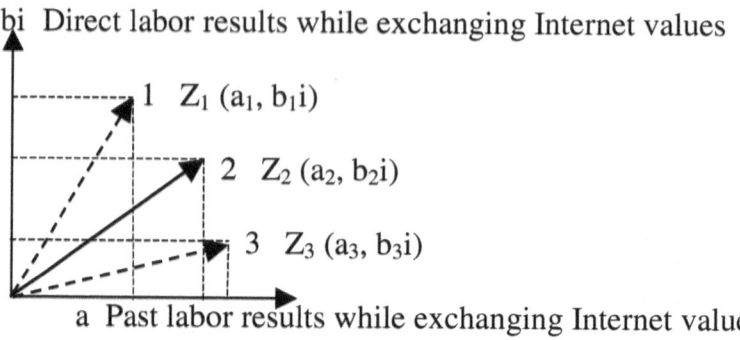

Where—a—past labor results while exchanging Internet values;
        bi—direct labor results while exchanging Internet values;
    Z(a + bi)—aggregate labor results while exchanging Internet
        values.

Vector Z takes the <u>first position</u> when the results of the exchange of
    direct labor are higher than those of past labor (while exchanging
    the Internet values)

Vector Z takes the third position when the results of the exchange of
    past labor are higher than those of direct labor during the
    exchange of Internet values.

In case of equality of the results of the exchange Vector Z is on a bisec-
    tor of angle φ—the second position.

2) Utilization of complex numbers while calculating the results of the
    Internet services.

CALCULATION OF RESULTS WHILE EXCHANGING INTERNET SERVICES WITH THE USE OF COMPLEX NUMBERS

1. Thesis   Past labor results while exchanging Internet services taking into account OLT resource (real number)

2. Antithesis   Direct labor results while exchanging Internet services taking into account OLT resource (imaginary number)

3. Synthesis   Aggregate results (indirect and direct) while exchanging Internet services taking into account OLT resource (a complex number)

The above can be shown graphically:

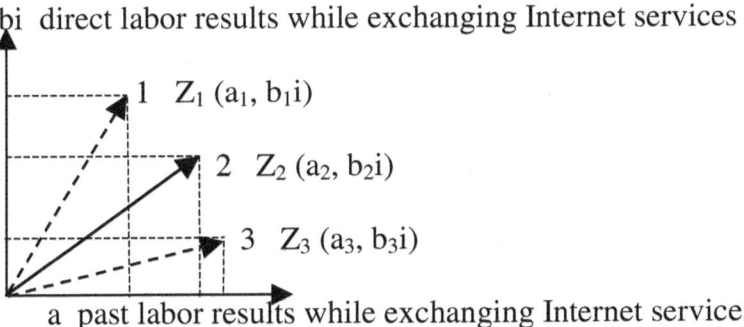

bi direct labor results while exchanging Internet services

1 $Z_1 (a_1, b_1 i)$

2 $Z_2 (a_2, b_2 i)$

3 $Z_3 (a_3, b_3 i)$

a past labor results while exchanging Internet services

where—a—past labor results while exchanging Internet services (real numbers);

bi—direct labor results while exchanging Internet services (imaginary numbers);

$Z(a + bi)$—aggregate labor results while exchanging Internet services (complex numbers).

Vector Z takes the <u>first position</u> when the results of the exchange of direct labor are higher than those of past labor (while exchanging the Internet services)

Vector Z takes the third position when the results of the exchange of past labor are higher than those of direct labor during the exchange of Internet services.

In case of equality of the results of the exchange Vector Z is on a bisector of angle φ—the second position.

The above can be written as follows:

1. Results while exchanging Internet values
2. Results while exchanging Internet services, taking into account a OLT resource
3. **Total:** Results while exchanging an Internet product: Internet values and services.

The above can also be written in the following way:

DIALECTICAL STRUCTURE
OF THE RESULTS DURING THE EXCHANGE OF A COMPLEX INTERNET PRODUCT TAKING INTO ACCOUNT OLT RESOURCE

THESIS
DIALECTICAL STRUCTURE
OF RESULT DURING THE EXCHANGE OF INTERNET VALUES

Thesis	Past labor results while exchanging Internet values
Antithesis	Direct labor results while exchanging Internet values
Synthesis	Aggregate labor results while exchanging Internet values

ANTITHESIS
DIALECTICAL STRUCTURE
OF RESULT DURING THE EXCHANGE OF IINTERNET SERVICES.

Thesis   Past labor results while exchanging Internet services, taking into account OLT resource

Antithesis   Direct labor results while exchanging Internet services, taking into account OLT resource

Synthesis   Aggregate labor results while exchanging Internet services, taking into account OLT resource

SYNTHESIS
DIALECTICAL STRUCTURE OF
RESULT WHILE EXCHANGING AN
AGGREGATE INTERNET PRODUCT

Thesis   Aggregate results of past labor participation while exchanging an «aggregate Internet product», taking into account OLT resource

Antithesis   Aggregate expenses from direct labor participation while exchanging an «aggregate Internet product», taking into account OLT resource

Synthesis   Aggregate results during the exchange of an «aggregate Internet product», taking into account A STP resource

Let us examine this problem in detail.

COMPLEX RESULTS CONNECTED TO THE MOVEMENT OF THE INTERNET PRODUCT WITHIN THE RELATIONS OF «EXCHANGE»

1) Thesis   Complex results of labor while exchanging Internet values (real numbers)

CALCULATION OF COMPLEX RESULTS OF THE INTERNET
VALUES WITHIN «EXCHANGE» RELATIONS

1st line—Thesis—estimation № 1
        Results of past labor while exchanging Internet values

2nd line—Antithesis—estimation № 2
        Results of direct labor while exchanging Internet values

3rd line—Synthesis—estimation № 3
        Aggregate results of labor while exchanging Internet values
        (complex number in complex number)—quaternion

2) Antithesis Complex results of labor while exchanging Internet services (real numbers)

CALCULATION OF COMPLEX RESULTS OF THE INTERNET
SERVICES WITHIN «EXCHANGE» RELATIONS

4st line—Thesis—estimation № 4
        Results of past labor while exchanging Internet services

5nd line—Antithesis—estimation № 5
        Results of direct labor while exchanging Internet services

6rd line—Synthesis—estimation № 6
        Aggregate results of labor while exchanging Internet services
        (complex number in complex number)—quaternion

3) Synthesis Aggregate results of labor of the Internet sphere while exchanging an Internet product (complex numbers)

CALCULATION OF COMPLEX RESULTS OF THE INTERNET PRODUCTS WITHIN «EXCHANGE» RELATIONS

7th line—Thesis—estimation № 7
Results of past labor while exchanging an Internet product, taking into account OLT resource

8th line—Antithesis—estimation № 8
Results of direct labor while exchanging an Internet product, taking into account OLT resource

9th line—Synthesis—estimation № 9
Aggregate results of labor while exchanging an Internet product, taking into account OLT resource (complex number in complex number)—quaternion.

The author examines these logic schemes to precisely ascertain where and which number is real; where and which number represents itself as an imaginary number; where and which value represents itself as a compound complex number.

Relations of exchange can be understood completely by considering the processes of reproduction of the Internet sphere. When the exchange is carried out not on an individual but at the general level of consideration, when in equalities and inequalities, pro-portions, participate, if it is right so, «big numbers», covering all process of an exchange.

D. COMPLEX RESULTS CONNECTED TO THE MOVEMENT OF THE INTERNET PRODUCT WITHIN THE RELATIONS OF «CONSUMPTION»

The movement of an Internet product begins with the phase of «production» and comes to an end in the «consumption» phase. This product goes through:

«production» → «distribution» → «exchange» → «consumption»

In its movement the Internet product breaks up into two components: movement of Internet values and movement of Internet services; which pass the same way:

Production		Distribution		Exchange		Consumption
Solitary «production» of Internet values	→	Solitary «distribution» of Internet values	→	Solitary «exchange» of Internet values	→	Solitary «consumption» of Internet values
↓		↓		↓		↓
Results within these economic relations	→	Results within these economic relations	→	Results within these economic relations	→	Results within these economic relations
Solitary «production» of Internet services	→	Solitary «distribution» of Internet services	→	Solitary «exchange» of Internet services	→	Solitary «consumption» of Internet services
↓		↓		↓		↓
Results within these economic relations	→	Results within these economic relations	→	Results within these economic relations	→	Results within these economic relations

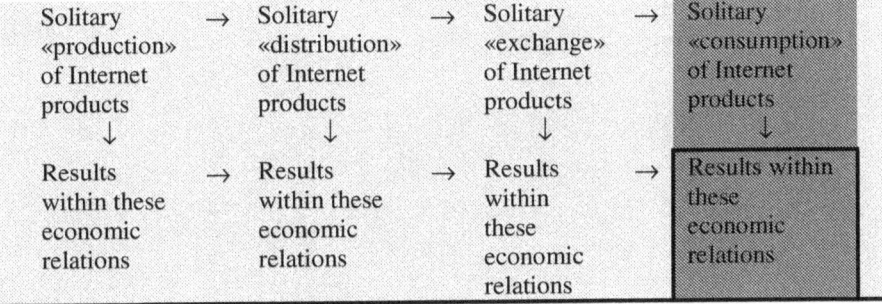

I am not going to compare the movement of Internet values and services to an athlete hurdling a 400 meter distance, but the results of economic movement of values and services will be different in every single case.

The necessity of studying the movement of the Internet product within the relations of «consumption» is stipulated by the fact that this process (production) is socially organized. This it first of all.

Second: the results of «consumption» are different, either good or bad. Here it would be necessary to study why increase or downfall of values in the results of consumption occur.

Within «consumption» relations there is a special result that differs from other economic results. Its essence is that inside the Internet sphere there is also the <u>non-production consumption, which is equal to the production consumption.</u> [15]

---

[15] The relation of «consumption» has internal and external aspects of consideration: internal and external consumption. Hence, the results of consumption will be different:

– result of «internal consumption» in the frames of Internet sphere;

– result of «external consumption» out of the frames of Internet sphere.

DUAL STRUCTURE OF
NEEDS IN THE INTERNET VALUE

Thesis   Production needs in Internet values (real needs)—a_1
Antithesis Non–production needs in Internet values—$b_1 i$
Synthesis   Complex needs in Internet values ($Z = a_1 + b_1 i$)

DUAL STRUCTURE OF
NEEDS IN THE INTERNET SERVICES

Thesis   Production needs in Internet services (real needs)—a_2
Antithesis Non–production needs in Internet services—$b_2 i$
Synthesis   Complex needs in Internet services ($Z_2 = a_2 + b_2 i$)

DUAL STRUCTURE
OF NEEDS IN THE INTERNET PRODUCT

Thesis   Production needs in Internet values and services (real numbers)—$(a_1 + a_2)$
Antithesis Non–production needs in Internet values and services (imaginary needs)—$(b_1 i + b_2 i)$
Synthesis   Complex needs in Internet values and services
$(Z_3 = (a_1 + a_2) + (b_1 i + b_2 i))$

1) Internet values: computers and software are used for production and non–production purposes. The above can be written down as:

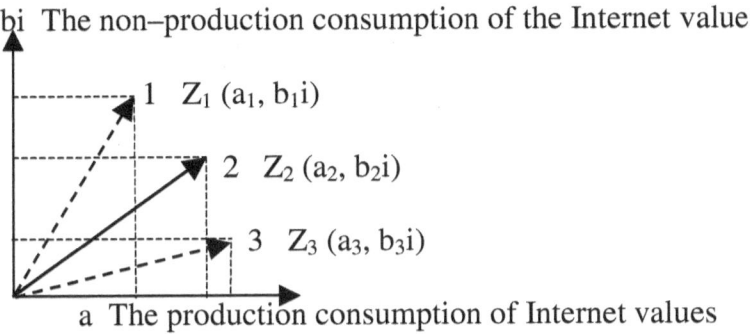

From—a—production consumption of Internet values

bi—non–production consumption of Internet values

$Z(a + bi)$—the aggregate (complex) consumption of Internet values

Results of consumption of the Internet values in the first, second, and third variants will be different.

Vector Z takes <u>position № 1</u> when the non-production consumption prevails over the production consumption of the Internet values.

Vector Z takes <u>position № 2</u> when the amounts of consumption of the Internet values having a production and non-production nature are equal.

The Vector Z takes <u>position № 3</u> if the production consumption of Internet values prevails over the non-production one.

2) The Internet services.

The results of consumption should be calculated by taking into account all resources involved in this process, including the human resource—«A»—visitors of the Internet sites.

The above can be interpreted graphically as:

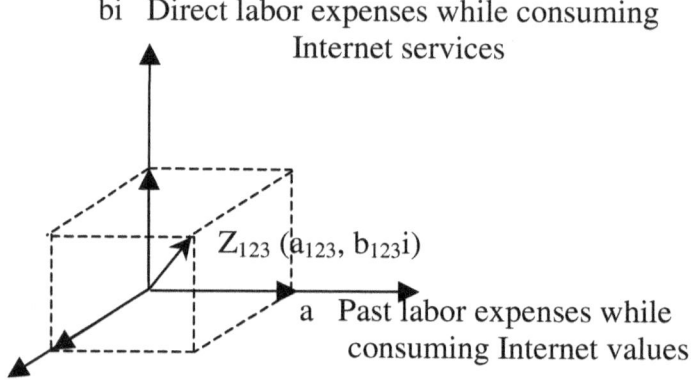

bi   Direct labor expenses while consuming Internet services

$Z_{123} (a_{123}, b_{123}i)$

a   Past labor expenses while consuming Internet values

Cj   Assimilated resource of time of the population

where—a—past labor expenses while consuming Internet values;
bi—direct labor expenses while consuming Internet services;
cj—assimilated resource of time of the population (A).

In case the third criterion—A—is absent, Vector $Z = a + bi$ will reflect complex expenses but not results. In this case we move to a two–dimensional space, where on the X axis there would be expenses—«a», while on the «Y» axis—expenses—bi.

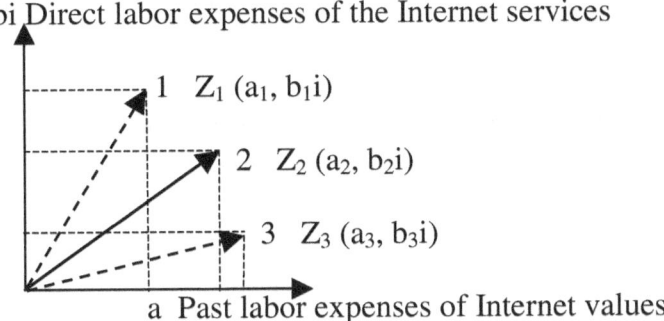

bi Direct labor expenses of the Internet services

1 $Z_1 (a_1, b_1i)$

2 $Z_2 (a_2, b_2i)$

3 $Z_3 (a_3, b_3i)$

a Past labor expenses of Internet values

If we take into account the nature of Internet sphere consumption—productive and non-productive—it may graphically be interpreted as follows:

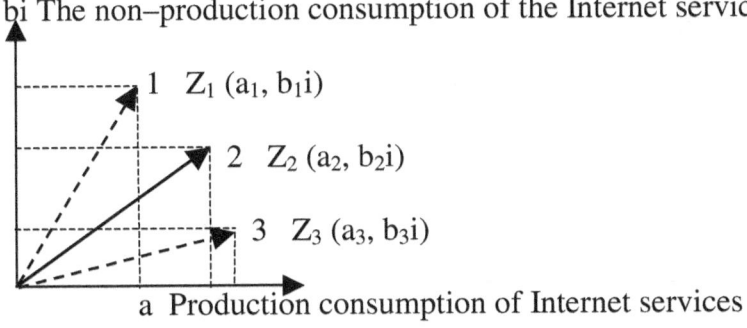

bi The non–production consumption of the Internet services

1 $Z_1 (a_1, b_1i)$

2 $Z_2 (a_2, b_2i)$

3 $Z_3 (a_3, b_3i)$

a Production consumption of Internet services

Where—a—production consumption of Internet services;
bi—non-production consumption of Internet services;
$Z (a + bi)$—aggregate (complex) consumption of Internet services.

Vector Z takes <u>position № 1</u> when the non-production consumption prevails over the production consumption of the Internet services.

Vector Z takes <u>position № 2</u> when the amounts of consumption of the
Internet services having a productive and non-productive nature
are equal.

The Vector Z takes <u>position № 3</u> if the production consumption of
Internet services prevails over the non-production one.

3) The Internet product

If we show the results connected to «consumption» of the Internet values on an axis of real numbers X, and the results connected to
«consumption» of the Internet services—on an axis Y, the number revealing the total results of the Internet sphere connected to
consumption can be written down as a complex number.[16]

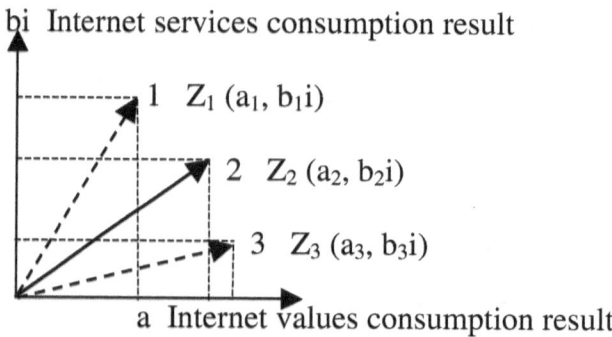

bi Internet services consumption result

1 $Z_1 (a_1, b_1 i)$

2 $Z_2 (a_2, b_2 i)$

3 $Z_3 (a_3, b_3 i)$

a Internet values consumption result

---

[16] Variant II

1. Thesis	Results of Internet values «consumption»—«a»
2. Antithesis	Results of Internet services «consumption», taking into account the assimilated resource «a»—(bi + cj)
3. Synthesis	Complex results of aggregate Internet product «consumption» $Z = a + bi + cj$ (look chapter 6)

Possible variants of consumption results:
- the first variant $Z_1 = a_1 + b_1i$ reflects the fact that within the relations of «consumption» the results connected to the Internet services prevail;
- in the second variant $Z_2 = a_2 + b_2i$: the results received within the relations of «consumption» of Internet values and services are equal;
- in the third variant $Z_3 = (a_1 + a_2) + (b_1i + b_2i)$ the results of «consumption» of Internet values prevail over the results connected to consumption of the Internet services.

The results of consumption will be different subject to the relations that exist between the components. This problem can be interpreted graphically as follows:

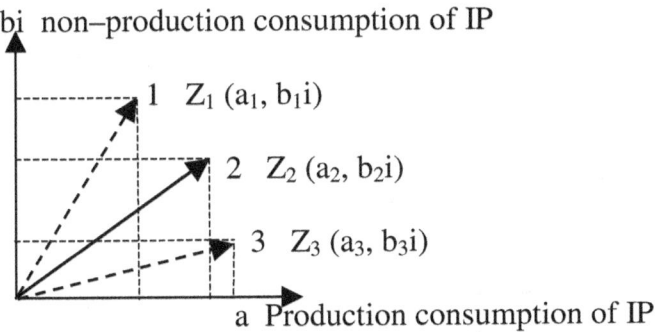

From a—production consumption of the Internet product;
bi—non-production consumption of the Internet product;
Z (a + bi)—aggregate (complex) consumption of the aggregate Internet product.

Vector Z takes <u>position № 1</u> when the non-production consumption prevails over the production consumption of the Internet product (IP).

Vector Z takes <u>position № 2</u> when the amount of consumption of the Internet products having a productive and non-productive nature are equal.

The Vector Z takes <u>position № 3</u> if the production consumption of Internet products prevails over the non-production one.

DIALECTICAL STRUCTURE
OF THE ECONOMIC RESULT CONNECTED TO «COMPLEX INTERNET PRODUCT» CONSUMPTION, TAKING INTO ACCOUNT OLT RESOURCE

THESIS

DIALECTICAL STRUCTURE
OF THE ECONOMIC RESULT OF INTERNET VALUES CONSUMPTION

Thesis	Economic results of Internet values «consumption» for production use (real number)—a_1
Antithesis	Economic results of Internet values «consumption» for non–production use (imaginary number)—$b_1 i$
Synthesis	Complex economic results of Internet values «consumption» for production and non–production use (complex number) $Z_1 = a_1 + b_1 i$

ANTITHESIS
DIALECTICAL STRUCTURE
OF THE ECONOMIC RESULT OF INTERNET SERVICES
CONSUMPTION

Thesis   Economic results of Internet services «consumption» for production use (real number)—a_2

Antithesis Economic results of Internet services «consumption» for non–production use (imaginary number)—b_2i

Synthesis   Complex economic results of Internet services «consumption» for production and non–production use (complex number) $Z_2 = a_2 + b_2i$

SYNTHESIS
DIALECTICAL STRUCTURE
OF THE ECONOMIC RESULT OF INTERNET PRODUCT
CONSUMPTION

Thesis   Economic results of Internet product «consumption» for production use (real number)—$(a_1 + a_2)$

Antithesis Economic results of Internet product «consumption» for non–production use (imaginary number)—$(b_1i + b_2i)$

Synthesis   Complex economic results of Internet product «consumption» for production and non–production use (complex number) $Z_3 = (a_1 + a_2) + (b_1i + b_2i)$

While considering the peculiarities of the economic results of movement of products of the Internet sphere within the relations of consumption we find that within a complex number there is another complex number. Let us examine this problem in detail.

CHAPTER 7. ECONOMIC INDICATORS OF THE INTERNET SPHERE

1. ECONOMIC INDICATORS OF THE INTERNET SPHERE WITH COMPLEX NUMBERS

2. BALANCE CORRELATIONS OF THE INTERNET SPHERE WITH COMPLEX NUMBERS

1. ECONOMIC INDICATORS OF THE INTERNET SPHERE WITH COMPLEX NUMBERS

Outlined generally production of Internet values and Internet services stands for:
- production of computers
- production of software programmes
- production of Internet services of manufacturing character taking into account the online time (OLT) of the Internat visitors working time;
- production of Internet services of educational character taking into account assimilated spare time of population (A_{STP});
- production of Internet services of enlightenment character also adjusted for A_{STP};
- production of Internet services of entertainment character also adjusted for A_{STP}.

These forms of activities are functionally dependent, supplementing one another. But taken separately they perform their own part in the general economic process of producing aggregate Internet values.

On this functional basis the forms of activities in question can be adapted to a system.

How to perform the formularized record of the Internet sphere? I suggest that it should be done with the use of complex numbers, or quaternions comprising several «imaginary» units.

In general, quaternions consisting of three components will be recordered as follows:

$$Z = a + bi + Cj$$

For four units the record is:

$$Z = a + bi + Cj + dk$$

where $i^2 = j^2 = k^2 = -1$

«Imaginary» numbers reveal different nature of origin of the number attached to them.

Proceeding from the presumption that economic product is comprised of three parts, namely;

C—past labor, V—direct labor, m—income, and that each of the above resource has different nature of origin, this circumstance makes it possible to use quaternions while formularizing indicators of the Internet sphere.

Indicator № 1—Economic estimate of the result of computer production:

$$R_1 = C_1 + V_1i + m_1j$$

Indicator № 2—Economic estimate of the result of output of the software programming products:

$$R_2 = C_2 + V_2i + m_2j$$

Economic estimate of the Internet service for the working part of the population is recorded as follows:

Indicator № 3—Internet services of productive purpose:

$$Z_1 = C_1 + V_1i + m_1j$$

Indicator № 4—Internet services of educational character:

$$Z_2 = C_1 + V_1 i + m_1 j + A^{ED}{}_{STP}K_2$$

Indicator № 5—Internet services of enlightenment character:

$$Z_3 = C_1 + V_1 i + m_1 j + A^{EN}{}_{STP}K_3$$

Indicator № 6—Internet services of entertainment character:

$$Z_4 = C_1 + V_1 i + m_1 j + A^{SH}{}_{STP}K_4$$

Using quaternions the Internet sphere can be introduced as follows:

$$\begin{cases} R_1 = C_1 + V_1 i + m_1 j \\[6pt] R_2 = C_2 + V_2 i + m_2 j \\[6pt] Z_1 = C_3 + V_3 i + m_3 j + Ok \\[6pt] Z_2 = C_4 + V_4 i + m_4 j + A^{ED}{}_{STP}k_2 \\[6pt] Z_3 = C_5 + V_5 i + m_5 j + A^{EN}{}_{STP}k_3 \\[6pt] Z_4 = C_6 + V_6 i + m_6 j + A^{SH}{}_{STP}k_4 \end{cases}$$

Where
m_1—income in I subdivision
m_2—income in II subdivision
m_3—paid online time of Internet visitors during working hours.

m_4, m_5, m_6,—paid online time of Internet visitors (A_{STP})
Ok, $A^{ED}_{STPk_2}$, $A^{EN}_{STPk_3}$, $A^{SH}_{STPk_4}$—unpaid, or economically non-estimated part of the assimilated spare time of population.

CALCULATION OF ECONOMIC INDICATORS OF THE INTERNET SPHERE

IP Division I

$C_1 + V_1 i + m_1 j$—GDP created in the Internet sphere (Subdivision I)
$V_1 i + m_1 j$—NDP created in the Internet sphere (Subdivision I)
$m_1 j$—NI created in the Internet sphere (Subdivision I)

IP Division II

$C_2 + V_2 i + m_2 j$—GDP created in the Internet sphere (Subdivision II)
$V_2 i + m_2 j$—NDP created in the Internet sphere (Subdivision II)

$m_2 j$—NI created in the Internet sphere (Subdivision II)

IP Division III

$C_3 + V_3 i + m_3 j + Ok$—GDP created in the Internet sphere (Subdivision III)

$V_3 i + m_3 j + Ok$—NDP created in the Internet sphere (Subdivision III)
$m_3 j + Ok$—NI created in the Internet sphere (Subdivision III)

Ok—assimilated resource STP within Subdivision III

IP Division IV

$C_4 + V_4 i + m_4 j + A^{ED}_{STPk_2}$—GDP created in the Internet sphere (Subdivision IV)

$V_4 i + m_4 j + A^{ED}_{STPk_2}$—NDP created in the Internet sphere (Subdivision IV)

$m_4 j + A^{ED}_{STPk_2}$—NI created in the Internet sphere (Subdivision IV)

$A^{ED}_{STPk_2}$—assimilated resource STP within Subdivision IV

IP Division V

$C_5 + V_5i + m_5j + A^{EN}_{STP}k_3$—GDP created in the Internet sphere (Subdivision V)

$V_5i + m_5j + A^{EN}_{STP}k_3$—NDP created in the Internet sphere (Subdivision V)

$m_5j + A^{EN}_{STP}k_3$—NI created in the Internet sphere (Subdivision V)

$A^{EN}_{STP}k_3$—assimilated resource STP within Subdivision V

IP Division VI

$C_6 + V_6i + m_6j + A^{SH}_{STP}k_4$—GDP created in the Internet sphere (Subdivision VI)

$V_6i + m_6j + A^{SH}_{STP}k_4$—NDP created in the Internet sphere (Subdivision VI)

$m_6j + A^{SH}_{STP}k_4$—NI created in the Internet sphere (Subdivision VI)

$A^{SH}_{STP}k_4$—assimilated resource STP within Subdivision VI

Calculation of GDP with the use of complex numbers

Subdivision I $GDP_1 = C_1 + V_1i + m_1j$
Subdivision II $GDP_2 = C_2 + V_2i + m_2j$
Subdivision III $GDP_3 = C_3 + V_3i + m_3j + Ok$
Subdivision IV $GDP_4 = C_4 + V_4i + m_4j + A^{ED}_{STP}k_2$
Subdivision V $GDP_5 = C_5 + V_5i + m_5j + A^{EN}_{STP}k_3$
Subdivision VI $GDP_6 = C_6 + V_6i + m_6j + A^{SH}_{STP}k_4$

$$Z_{GDP} = C_1 + V_1i + m_1j + C_2 + V_2i + m_2j + C_3 + V_3i + m_3j + Ok + C_4 + V_4i + m_4j + A^{ED}_{STP}k_2 + C_5 + V_5i + m_5j + A^{EN}_{STP}k_3 + C_6 + V_6i + m_6j + A^{SH}_{STP}k_4$$

Calculation of NDP

Subdivision I $NDP_1 = V_1 i + m_1 j$

Subdivision II $NDP_2 = V_2 i + m_2 j$

Subdivision III $NDP_3 = V_3 i + m_3 j + Ok$

Subdivision IV $NDP_4 = V_4 i + m_4 j + A^{ED}_{STP} k_2$

Subdivision V $NDP_5 = V_5 i + m_5 j + A^{EN}_{STP} k_3$

Subdivision VI $NDP_6 = V_6 i + m_6 j + A^{SH}_{STP} k_4$

$Z_{NDP} = V_1 i + m_1 j + V_2 i + m_2 j + V_3 i + m_3 j + Ok + V_4 i + m_4 j + A^{ED}_{STP} k_2 + V_5 i + m_5 j + A^{EN}_{STP} k_3 + V_6 i + m_6 j + A^{SH}_{STP} k_4$

Calculation of NI

Subdivision I $NI_1 = m_1 j$

Subdivision II $NI_2 = m_2 j$

Subdivision III $NI_3 = m_3 j + Ok$

Subdivision IV $NI_4 = m_4 j + A^{ED}_{STP} k_2$

Subdivision V $NI_5 = m_5 j + A^{EN}_{STP} k_3$

Subdivision VI $NI_6 = m_6 j + A^{SH}_{STP} k_4$

$Z_{NI} = m_1 j + m_2 j + m_3 j + Ok + m_4 j + A^{ED}_{STP} k_2 + m_5 j + A^{EN}_{STP} k_3 + m_6 j + A^{SH}_{STP} k_4$

Calculation of A_{STP}

Subdivision III $A_{STP} = Ok$

Subdivision IV $A_{STP} = A^{ED}_{STP} k_2$

Subdivision V $A_{STP} = A^{EN}_{STP} k_3$

Subdivision VI $A_{STP} = A^{SH}_{STP} k_4$

Total: $Ok + A^{ED}_{STP} k_2 + A^{EN}_{STP} k_3 + A^{SH}_{STP} k_4$

2. BALANCE CORRELATION OF THE INTERNET SPHERE WITH COMPLEX NUMBERS

One of the key questions of the Internet sphere is what proportions are sustained in the process of its functioning? Here we may deal with several options:

- if proportion among the segments of Internet values, services and aggregate Internet product correlates with the logic of reproduction in this sphere, the results will be of one kind. They will rest within the spectrum of positive trends;

- if proportion among the segments of Internet values, services and aggregate Internet product are not sustained the results of the Internet sphere movement in the economic space will be negative.

Scheme A Variant I

$$
\text{The Internet Production}
\begin{cases}
\text{Division 1}
\begin{cases}
C_1 + \boxed{v_1 i + m_1 j} - R_1 & \text{Subdivision 1} \\
C_2 + \boxed{v_2 i + m_2 j} - R_2 & \text{Subdivision 2}
\end{cases} \\
\qquad\qquad |<| \\
\text{Division 2}
\begin{cases}
\boxed{C_3} + v_3 i + m_3 j + Ok - Z_1 & \text{Subdivision 3} \\
\boxed{C_4} + v_4 i + m_4 j + A^{ED}{}_{STP} k_2 - Z_2 & \text{Subdivision 4} \\
\boxed{C_5} + v_5 i + m_5 j + A^{EN}{}_{STP} k_3 - Z_3 & \text{Subdivision 5} \\
\boxed{C_6} + v_6 i + m_6 j + A^{SH}{}_{STP} k_4 - Z_4 & \text{Subdivision 6}
\end{cases}
\end{cases}
$$

$$\left.\begin{array}{l} \text{I} \ (C_1 + V_1i + m_1j) \\[2em] \text{II} \ (C_2 + V_2i + m_2j) \end{array}\right\} > (C_1 + C_2 + C_3 + C_4 + C_5 + C_6)$$

or

$$\left.\begin{array}{l} \text{I} \ (V_1i + m_1j) \\[2em] \text{II} \ (V_2i + m_2j) \end{array}\right\} > (C_3 + C_4 + C_5 + C_6)$$

or

$$\text{I} \ (V_1i + m_1j) + \text{II} \ (V_2i + m_2j) - (C_3 + C_4 + C_5 + C_6) > 0$$

Scheme A Variant II

The Internet Production

Division 1
- $C_1 + \boxed{V_1i + m_1j} - R_1$ Subdivision 1
- $C_2 + \boxed{V_2i + m_2j} - R_2$ Subdivision 2

$|<|$

Division 2
- $C_3 + V_3j + m_3j + Ok - Z_1$ Subdivision 3
- $C_4 + V_4j + m_4j + A^{KD}_{GTP}k_2 - Z_2$ Subdivision 4
- $C_5 + V_5j + m_5j + A^{EN}_{STP}k_3 - Z_3$ Subdivision 5
- $C_6 + V_6j + m_6j + A^{SH}_{STP}k_4 - Z_4$ Subdivision 6

$$\left.\begin{array}{l} \text{I } (C_1 + V_1 i + m_1 j) \\[20pt] \text{II } (C_2 + V_2 i + m_2 j) \end{array}\right\} > (C_1 + C_2 + C_3 + C_4 + C_5)$$

or

$$\left.\begin{array}{l} \text{I } (V_1 i + m_1 j) \\[20pt] \text{II } (V_2 i + m_2 j) \end{array}\right\} > (C_3 + C_4 + C_5)$$

or

$$\text{I } (V_1 i + m_1 j) + \text{II } (V_2 i + m_2 j) - (C_3 + C_4 + C_5) > 0$$

Scheme A Variant III

$$\text{The Internet Production} \left\{ \begin{array}{l} \text{Division 1} \left\{ \begin{array}{ll} C_1 + \boxed{V_1 i + m_1 j} - R_1 & \text{Subdivision 1} \\ C_2 + \boxed{V_2 i + m_2 j} - R_2 & \text{Subdivision 2} \end{array} \right. \\[10pt] \qquad\qquad |<| \\[10pt] \text{Division 2} \left\{ \begin{array}{ll} \boxed{C_3} + V_3 i + m_3 j + Ok - Z_1 & \text{Subdivision 3} \\ \boxed{C_4} + V_4 i + m_4 j + A^{KD}_{STP} k_2 - Z_2 & \text{Subdivision 4} \\ C_5 + V_5 i + m_5 j + A^{EN}_{STP} k_3 - Z_3 & \text{Subdivision 5} \\ C_6 + V_6 i + m_6 j + A^{III}_{STP} k_4 - Z_4 & \text{Subdivision 6} \end{array} \right. \end{array} \right.$$

$$\left.\begin{array}{l} \text{I } (C_1 + V_1i + m_1j) \\[20pt] \text{II } (C_2 + V_2i + m_2j) \end{array}\right\} > (C_1 + C_2 + C_3 + C_4)$$

or

$$\left.\begin{array}{l} \text{I } (V_1i + m_1j) \\[20pt] \text{II } (V_2i + m_2j) \end{array}\right\} > (C_3 + C_4)$$

or

$$\text{I } (V_1i + m_1j) + \text{II } (V_2i + m_2j) - (C_3 + C_4) > 0$$

Scheme A Variant IV

$$\left. \begin{array}{l} \text{I } (C_1 + V_1i + m_1j) \\[2em] \text{II } (C_2 + V_2i + m_2j) \end{array} \right\} > (C_1 + C_2 + C_3)$$

or

$$\left. \begin{array}{l} \text{I } (V_1i + m_1j) \\[2em] \text{II } (V_2i + m_2j) \end{array} \right\} > C_3$$

or

$$\text{I } (V_1i + m_1j) + \text{II } (V_2i + m_2j) - C_3 > 0$$

Scheme B Variant I

$$\left. \begin{array}{l} \text{I } (C_1 + V_1 i + m_1 j) \\[2em] \text{II } (C_2 + V_2 i + m_2 j) \end{array} \right\} = (C_1 + C_2 + C_3 + C_4 + C_5 + C_6)$$

or

$$\left. \begin{array}{l} \text{I } (V_1 i + m_1 j) \\[2em] \text{II } (V_2 i + m_2 j) \end{array} \right\} = (C_3 + C_4 + C_5 + C_6)$$

or

$$\text{I } (V_1 i + m_1 j) + \text{II } (V_2 i + m_2 j) - (C_3 + C_4 + C_5 + C_6) = 0$$

Scheme B Variant II

$$\left.\begin{array}{l} \text{I } (C_1 + V_1 i + m_1 j) \\[2em] \text{II } (C_2 + V_2 i + m_2 j) \end{array}\right\} = (C_1 + C_2 + C_3 + C_4 + C_5)$$

or

$$\left.\begin{array}{l} \text{I } (V_1 i + m_1 j) \\[2em] \text{II } (V_2 i + m_2 j) \end{array}\right\} = (C_3 + C_4 + C_5)$$

or

$$\text{I } (V_1 i + m_1 j) + \text{II } (V_2 i + m_2 j) - (C_3 + C_4 + C_5) = 0$$

Scheme B Variant III

$$\text{The Internet Production} \left\{\begin{array}{l} \text{Division 1} \left\{\begin{array}{ll} C_1 + \boxed{V_1 i + m_1 j} - R_1 & \text{Subdivision 1} \\ C_2 + \boxed{V_2 i + m_2 j} - R_2 & \text{Subdivision 2} \end{array}\right. \\[1em] \hspace{2cm} |=| \\[1em] \text{Division 2} \left\{\begin{array}{ll} \boxed{C_3} + V_3 i + m_3 j + Qk - X_1 & \text{Subdivision 3} \\ \boxed{C_4} + V_4 i + m_4 j + A^{KO}{}_{STP}k_2 - X_2 & \text{Subdivision 4} \\ C_5 + V_5 i + m_5 j + A^{EN}{}_{STP}k_3 - Z_3 & \text{Subdivision 5} \\ C_6 + V_6 i + m_6 j + A^{SII}{}_{STP}k_4 - X_4 & \text{Subdivision 6} \end{array}\right. \end{array}\right.$$

$$\left.\begin{array}{l} \text{I } (C_1 + V_1 i + m_1 j) \\[2em] \text{II } (C_2 + V_2 i + m_2 j) \end{array}\right\} = (C_1 + C_2 + C_3 + C_4)$$

or

$$\left.\begin{array}{l} \text{I } (V_1 i + m_1 j) \\[2em] \text{II } (V_2 i + m_2 j) \end{array}\right\} = (C_3 + C_4)$$

or

$$\text{I } (V_1 i + m_1 j) + \text{II } (V_2 i + m_2 j) - (C_3 + C_4) = 0$$

Scheme B Variant IV

$$\text{The Internet Production}\left\{\begin{array}{l} \text{Division 1}\begin{cases} C_1 + \boxed{V_1 i + m_1 j} - R_1 \qquad \text{Subdivision 1} \\ C_2 + \boxed{V_2 i + m_2 j} - R_2 \qquad \text{Subdivision 2} \end{cases} \\ \qquad\qquad\qquad |=| \\ \text{Division 2}\begin{cases} \boxed{C_3} + V_3 i + m_3 j + Ok - X_1 \qquad \text{Subdivision 3} \\ C_4 + V_4 i + m_4 j + A^{RD}_{STPK_2} - X_2 \quad \text{Subdivision 4} \\ C_5 + V_5 i + m_5 j + A^{EN}_{STPK_3} - Z_3 \quad \text{Subdivision 5} \\ C_6 + V_6 i + m_6 j + A^{SH}_{STPK_4} - X_4 \quad \text{Subdivision 6} \end{cases} \end{array}\right.$$

$$\left. \begin{array}{l} \text{I } (C_1 + V_1i + m_1j) \\[2em] \text{II } (C_2 + V_2i + m_2j) \end{array} \right\} = (C_1 + C_2 + C_3)$$

or

$$\left. \begin{array}{l} \text{I } (V_1i + m_1j) \\[2em] \text{II } (V_2i + m_2j) \end{array} \right\} = C_3$$

or

$$\text{I } (V_1i + m_1j) + \text{II } (V_2i + m_2j) - C_3 = 0$$

Scheme C Variant I

The Internet Production

Division 1
$C_1 + \boxed{V_1i + m_1j} - R_1$ Subdivision 1
$C_2 + \boxed{V_2i + m_2j} - R_2$ Subdivision 2

Division 2
$C_3 + V_3i + m_3j + Ok - Z_1$ Subdivision 3
$C_4 + V_4i + m_4j + A^{KD}_{STPk}k_2 - Z_2$ Subdivision 4
$C_5 + V_5i + m_5j + A^{EN}_{STPk}k_3 - Z_3$ Subdivision 5
$C_6 + V_6i + m_6j + A^{III}_{STPk}k_4 - Z_4$ Subdivision 6

$$\left.\begin{array}{l} \text{I } (C_1 + V_1i + m_1j) \\[2em] \text{II } (C_2 + V_2i + m_2j) \end{array}\right\} < (C_1 + C_2 + C_3 + C_4 + C_5 + C_6)$$

or

$$\left.\begin{array}{l} \text{I } (V_1i + m_1j) \\[2em] \text{II } (V_2i + m_2j) \end{array}\right\} < (C_3 + C_4 + C_5 + C_6)$$

or

$$\text{I } (V_1i + m_1j) + \text{II } (V_2i + m_2j) - (C_3 + C_4 + C_5 + C_6) < 0$$

Scheme C Variant II

$$
\begin{array}{l}
\text{The Internet}\\
\text{Production}
\end{array}
\left\{
\begin{array}{l}
\text{Division 1}\left\{
\begin{array}{ll}
C_1 + \boxed{V_1i + m_1j} - R_1 & \text{Subdivision 1}\\
C_2 + \boxed{V_2i + m_2j} - R_2 & \text{Subdivision 2}
\end{array}\right.\\[3em]
\text{Division 2}\left\{
\begin{array}{ll}
C_3 + V_3i + m_3j + Ok - Z_1 & \text{Subdivision 3}\\
C_4 + V_4i + m_4j + A^{KD}_{STP}k_2 - Z_2 & \text{Subdivision 4}\\
C_5 + V_5i + m_5j + A^{EN}_{STP}k_3 - Z_3 & \text{Subdivision 5}\\
C_6 + V_6i + m_6j + A^{SH}_{STP}k_4 - Z_4 & \text{Subdivision 6}
\end{array}\right.
\end{array}
\right.
$$

$$\left.\begin{array}{l} \text{I } (C_1 + V_1 i + m_1 j) \\[2em] \text{II } (C_2 + V_2 i + m_2 j) \end{array}\right\} < (C_1 + C_2 + C_3 + C_4 + C_5)$$

or

$$\left.\begin{array}{l} \text{I } (V_1 i + m_1 j) \\[2em] \text{II } (V_2 i + m_2 j) \end{array}\right\} < (C_3 + C_4 + C_5)$$

or

$$\text{I } (V_1 i + m_1 j) + \text{II } (V_2 i + m_2 j) - (C_3 + C_4 + C_5) < 0$$

Scheme C Variant III

The Internet Production

Division 1
- $C_1 + \boxed{V_1 i + m_1 j} - R_1$ Subdivision 1
- $C_2 + \boxed{V_2 i + m_2 j} - R_2$ Subdivision 2

$|>|$

Division 2
- $\boxed{C_3} + V_3 i + m_3 j + Ok - X_1$ Subdivision 3
- $\boxed{C_4} + V_4 i + m_4 j + A^{ED}_{STP} k_2 - X_2$ Subdivision 4
- $C_5 + V_5 i + m_5 j + A^{IN}_{STP} k_3 - Z_3$ Subdivision 5
- $C_6 + V_6 i + m_6 j + A^{SH}_{STP} k_4 - X_4$ Subdivision 6

$$\left.\begin{array}{l} \text{I } (C_1 + V_1 i + m_1 j) \\[2em] \text{II } (C_2 + V_2 i + m_2 j) \end{array}\right\} < (C_1 + C_2 + C_3 + C_4)$$

or

$$\left.\begin{array}{l} \text{I } (V_1 i + m_1 j) \\[2em] \text{II } (V_2 i + m_2 j) \end{array}\right\} < (C_3 + C_4)$$

or

$$\text{I } (V_1 i + m_1 j) + \text{II } (V_2 i + m_2 j) - (C_3 + C_4) < 0$$

Scheme C Variant IV

The Internet Production

$$\left\{\begin{array}{l}
\text{Division 1}
\left\{\begin{array}{ll}
C_1 + \boxed{V_1 i + m_1 j} - R_1 & \text{Subdivision 1} \\
C_2 + \boxed{V_2 i + m_2 j} - R_2 & \text{Subdivision 2}
\end{array}\right. \\[1em]
\qquad\qquad\qquad |>| \\[1em]
\text{Division 2}
\left\{\begin{array}{ll}
\boxed{C_3} + V_3 i + m_3 j + Qk - Z_1 & \text{Subdivision 3} \\
C_4 + V_4 i + m_4 j + A^{BD}_{STP} k_2 - Z_2 & \text{Subdivision 4} \\
C_5 + V_5 i + m_5 j + A^{EN}_{STP} k_3 - Z_3 & \text{Subdivision 5} \\
C_6 + V_6 i + m_6 j + A^{GH}_{STP} k_4 - Z_4 & \text{Subdivision 6}
\end{array}\right.
\end{array}\right.$$

$$\left.\begin{array}{l} \text{I } (C_1 + V_1 i + m_1 j) \\[2em] \text{II } (C_2 + V_2 i + m_2 j) \end{array}\right\} < (C_1 + C_2 + C_3)$$

or

$$\left.\begin{array}{l} \text{I } (V_1 i + m_1 j) \\[2em] \text{II } (V_2 i + m_2 j) \end{array}\right\} < C_3$$

or

$$\text{I } (V_1 i + m_1 j) + \text{II } (V_2 i + m_2 j) - C_3 < 0$$

CHAPTER 8. SYSTEM OF CRITERIA REFLECTING THE MOVEMENT OF INTERNET VALUES AND INTERNET SERVICES (WITH COMPLEX NUMBERS—QUATERNIONS)

The movement of Internet values, Internet services as well as of the aggregate Internet product occurs within four economic media: production, distribution, exchange and consumption.

Estimates of the movement should certainly be made for each economic area.

Different economic media—different rate of movement—different values of economic estimates.

The movement of Internet values and Internet services occurs not only in the frames of the sphere itself, but beyond its boundaries as well.

In this connection we shall establish criteria of movement at all stages and every economic medium:

Table № 1

	Production	Distribution	Exchange	Consumption
Results	Economic results of the movement of Internet values in the frames production	Economic results of the movement of Internet values in the frames distribution	Economic results of the movement of Internet values in the frames exchange	Economic results of the movement of Internet values in the frames consumption
Expenses	Economic expenses of the movement of Internet values in the frames production	Economic expenses of the movement of Internet values in the frames distribution	Economic expenses of the movement of Internet values in the frames exchange	Economic expenses of the movement of Internet values in the frames consumption
Criteria	Economic criteria of the movement of Internet values in the frames production	Economic criteria of the movement of Internet values in the frames distribution	Economic criteria of the movement of Internet values in the frames exchange	Economic criteria of the movement of Internet values in the frames consumption

Table № 2

	Production	Distribution	Exchange	Consumption
Results	Economic results of the movement of Internet services in the frames production	Economic results of the movement of Internet services in the frames distribution	Economic results of the movement of Internet services in the frames exchange	Economic results of the movement of Internet services in the frames consumption
Expenses	Economic expenses of the movement of Internet services in the frames production	Economic expenses of the movement of Internet services in the frames distribution	Economic expenses of the movement of Internet services in the frames exchange	Economic expenses of the movement of Internet services in the frames consumption
Criteria	Economic criteria of the movement of Internet services in the frames production	Economic criteria of the movement of Internet services in the frames distribution	Economic criteria of the movement of Internet services in the frames exchange	Economic criteria of the movement of Internet services in the frames consumption

Table № 3

	Production	Distribution	Exchange	Consumption
Results	Economic results of the movement of Internet product in the frames production	Economic results of the movement of Internet product in the frames distribution	Economic results of the movement of Internet product in the frames exchange	Economic results of the movement of Internet product in the frames consumption
Expenses	Economic expenses of the movement of Internet product in the frames production	Economic expenses of the movement of Internet product in the frames distribution	Economic expenses of the movement of Internet product in the frames exchange	Economic expenses of the movement of Internet product in the frames consumption
Criteria	Economic criteria of the movement of Internet product in the frames production	Economic criteria of the movement of Internet product in the frames distribution	Economic criteria of the movement of Internet product in the frames exchange	Economic criteria of the movement of Internet product in the frames consumption

1. CRITERIA OF RESOURCE UTILIZATION WITHIN SUBDIVISION 1 OF THE INTERNET SPHERE

Internet values being placed in the three-dimensional space appear as follows:

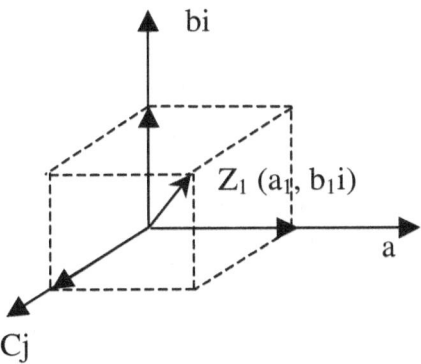

where a—past labor expenses;
   bi—direct labor expenses;
   mj—income.

AA) ECONOMIC CRITERION № 1 REFLECTING THE MOVEMENT OF INTERNET VALUES

$$\text{Result/Expenses} = \frac{\text{Result—Economic estimate of the Internet values in three-dimensional space}}{\text{Past labor expenses}}$$

Formularized written criterion:

$$AA = \frac{a + bi + mj}{a}$$

This criteria allows to establish the trajectory of movement of Internet values in section «a».

BB) ECONOMIC CRITERION № 2 REFLECTING THE MOVE-MENT OF INTERNET VALUES

$$\text{Result/Expenses} = \frac{\text{Result—Economic estimate of the Internet values in three-dimensional space}}{\text{Direct labor expenses}}$$

Formularized written criterion:

$$BB = \frac{a + bi + mj}{bi}$$

This criteria allows to establish the trajectory of movement of Internet values in section «b».

CC) AGGREGATE ECONOMIC CRITERION № 3 REFLECTING THE MOVEMENT OF INTERNET VALUES

$$\text{Result/Expenses} = \frac{\text{Result—Economic estimate of the Internet values in three-dimensional space}}{\text{Aggregate labor expenses}}$$

Formularized written criterion:

$$CC = \frac{a + bi + mj}{bi}$$

DD) CRITERIA VARIETY REFLECTING THE MOVEMENT OF INTERNET VALUES

1. Proportionate correlation of GDP represented in three-dimensional space with past labor expenses produces the following criteria:

$$AA_1 = \frac{a + bi + mj}{\text{Past labor expenses}} = \frac{a + bi + mj}{a} = \frac{GDP}{a}$$

2. In this variant below we calculate NDP represented in two-dimensional space, in proportion with past labor expenses.

$$AA_2 = \frac{bi + mj}{\text{Past labor expenses}} = \frac{bi + mj}{a} = \frac{NDP}{a}$$

3. And the last variant below reveals correlation of NI in proportion with past labor expenses.

$$AA_3 = \frac{mj}{\text{Past labor expenses}} = \frac{mj}{a} = \frac{NI}{a}$$

2) The above noted criteria may be supplemented by the following:

In the frames of this criterion we proportionately correlate GDP Internet values represented in three-dimensional space with direct labor expenses.

$$BB_1 = \frac{a + bi + mj}{\text{Direct labor expenses}} = \frac{a + bi + mj}{bi} = \frac{GDP}{bi}$$

In this variant we correlate NDP, represented in two-dimensional space, in proportion with direct labor expenses.

$$BB_2 = \frac{bi + mj}{\text{Direct labor expenses}} = \frac{bi + mj}{bi} = \frac{GDP}{bi}$$

In this variant we correlate NI with direct labor expenses.

$$BB_3 = \frac{mj}{\text{Direct labor expenses}} = \frac{mj}{bi} = \frac{NI}{bi}$$

The above given criteria may be supplemented by:

3) Integrating (complex) criteria reflecting the movement of Internet values.

$$CC_1 = \frac{a + bi + mj}{\text{Aggregate labor expenses}} = \frac{a + bi + mj}{a + bi} = \frac{\text{GDP}}{a + bi}$$

$$CC_2 = \frac{bi + mj}{\text{Aggregate labor expenses}} = \frac{bi + mj}{a + bi} = \frac{\text{NDP}}{a + bi}$$

$$CC_3 = \frac{mj}{\text{Aggregate labor expenses}} = \frac{mj}{a + bi} = \frac{\text{NI}}{a + bi}$$

A distinguishing feature of AA1, BB1, CC1 criteria is that we correlate economic indicators represented by quaternions, in proportion with expenses recorded as complex numbers.

$$K = \frac{\text{Quaternion}}{\text{Complex number}}$$

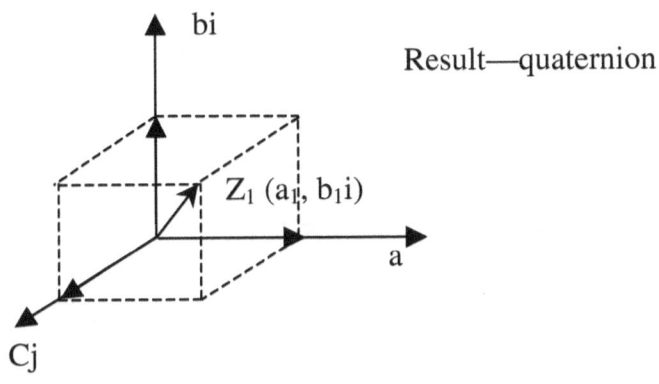

Result—quaternion

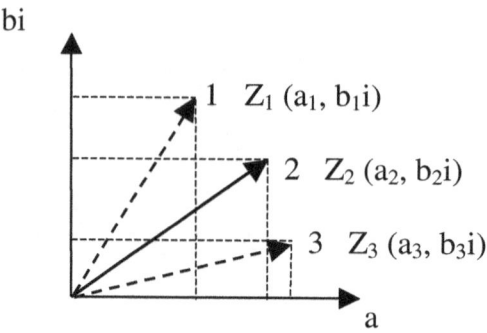

2. ECONOMIC CRITERIA REFLECTING THE MOVEMENT OF INTERNET SERVICE

In the three-dimensional space Internet service can be drawn as follows:

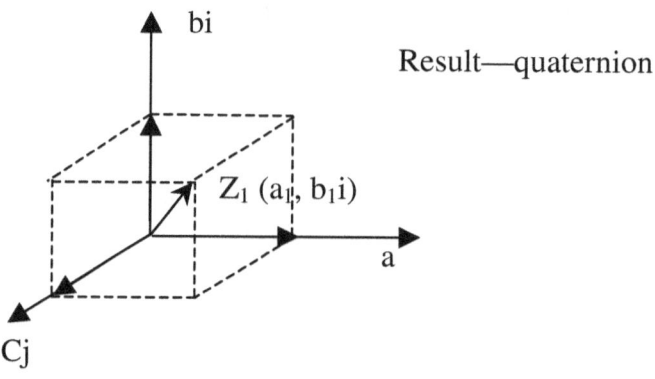

where a—past labor expenses;
    bi—direct labor expenses;
    Cj—assimilated time of Internet visitors.

All resources are placed on different «X», «Y», «Z» axes, due to their heterogeneity R = a + bi + Cj.

R—vector reveals the total cost of Internet service adjusted for the assimilated and economically evaluated Internet visitor time resource.

At the second stage we shall consider the correlation of results and expenses connected to the movement of Internet services.

AA) ECONOMIC CRITERION № 1 REFLECTING THE MOVEMENT OF INTERNET SERVICES

$$\text{Result/Expenses} = \frac{\text{Result—Economic estimate of the Internet services in three-dimensional space}}{\text{Past labor expenses}}$$

Formularized written criterion:

$$K_1 = \frac{a + bi + Cj}{a}$$

The criterion makes it possible to establish the trajectory of movement of Internet resource in «a» selection.

BB) ECONOMIC CRITERION № 2 REFLECTING THE MOVE-MENT OF INTERNET SERVICES

$$\text{Result/Expenses} = \frac{\text{Result—Economic estimate of the Internet services in three-dimensional space}}{\text{Direct labor expenses}}$$

Formularized written criterion:

$$K_2 = \frac{a + bi + Cj}{bi}$$

This criterion makes it possible to establish the trajectory of movement of Internet resource in «b» selection.

CC) AGGREGATE ECONOMIC CRITERION № 3 REFLECTING THE MOVEMENT OF INTERNET SERVICES

$$\text{Result/Expenses} = \frac{\text{Result—Economic estimate of the Internet services in three-dimensional space}}{\text{Aggregate labor expenses}}$$

Formularized written criterion:

$$K_3 = \frac{a + bi + Cj}{a + bi}$$

This criteria allows to establish general trajectory of movement of Internet resources.

While estimating these criteria it is necessary to proceed from algebraic rules on complex numbers.

$$K = \frac{\text{Quaternion}}{\text{Complex number}}$$

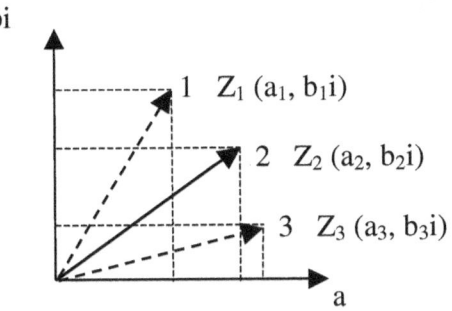

Result—quaternion

$Z_1 (a_1, b_1 i)$

Expenses—Complex number

$1 \quad Z_1 (a_1, b_1 i)$

$2 \quad Z_2 (a_2, b_2 i)$

$3 \quad Z_3 (a_3, b_3 i)$

DD) CRITERIA VARIETY REFLECTING THE MOVEMENT OF INTERNET SERVICES

Proportionate correlation of GDP referred to the service part of Internet sphere within three-dimensional space with that past of labor expenses:

$$A_1 = \frac{a + bi + Cj}{\text{Past labor expenses}} = \frac{a + bi + Cj}{a} = \frac{GDP}{a}$$

Proportionate correlation of NDP with past of labor expenses:

$$A_2 = \frac{bi + Cj}{\text{Past labor expenses}} = \frac{bi + Cj}{a} = \frac{NDP}{a}$$

Proportionate correlation of NI with past of labor expenses:

$$A_2 = \frac{Cj}{\text{Past labor expenses}} = \frac{Cj}{a} = \frac{NI}{a}$$

Apart from the noted there is another set of criteria within which the results of movement of Internet service are correlated with the direct labor expenses in proportion.

Proportionate correlation of GDP represented in three-dimensional space with direct labor expenses.

$$B_1 = \frac{a + bi + Cj}{\text{Direct labor expenses}} = \frac{a + bi + Cj}{bi} = \frac{\text{GDP}}{bi}$$

In this criterion NDP represented in two-dimensional space and direct labor expenses are correlated in proportion:

$$B_2 = \frac{bi + Cj}{\text{Direct labor expenses}} = \frac{bi + Cj}{bi} = \frac{\text{NDP}}{bi}$$

Within this criterion we can correlate NI in proportion with the direct labor expenses.

$$B_3 = \frac{Cj}{\text{Direct labor expenses}} = \frac{Cj}{bi} = \frac{\text{NI}}{bi}$$

Along with the above-mentioned criteria there are also integrating ones with the expense part including past and real labor (a + bi).

$$C_1 = \frac{a + bi + Cj}{\text{Aggregate labor expenses}} = \frac{a + bi + Cj}{a + bi} = \frac{\text{GDP}}{a + bi}$$

$$C_2 = \frac{bi + Cj}{\text{Aggregate labor expenses}} = \frac{bi + Cj}{a + bi} = \frac{\text{NDP}}{a + bi}$$

$$C_3 = \frac{Cj}{\text{Aggregate labor expenses}} = \frac{Cj}{a + bi} = \frac{\text{NI}}{a + bi}$$

3. COMPLEX ECONOMIC CRITERIA REFLECTING THE MOVEMENT OF INTERNET PRODUCT

Economic criterion № 1

$$\text{Result/Expenses} = \frac{\text{Result—Economic estimate of aggregate Internet product in three-dimensional space}}{\text{Past labor expenses}}$$

Formularized writing of the criterion:

$$AAA = \frac{a_1 + b_1 i + m_1 j + a_2 + b_2 i + C_2 j}{a_1 + a_2} = \frac{GDP_1 + GDP_2}{a_1 + a_2}$$

where

$a_1 + b_1 + m_1 j$—GDP of Internet values

$a_2 + b_2 + C_2 j$—GDP of Internet services

Economic criterion № 2

$$\text{Result/Expenses} = \frac{\text{Result— Economic estimate of aggregate Internet product in three-dimensional space}}{\text{Direct labor expenses}}$$

Formularized writing of the criterion:

$$BBB = \frac{a_1 + b_1 i + m_1 j + a_2 + b_2 i + C_2 j}{b_1 i + b_2 i} = \frac{GDP_1 + GDP_2}{b_1 i + b_2 i}$$

Economic criterion № 3

$$\text{Result/Expenses} = \frac{\text{Result—Economic estimate of aggregate Internet product in three-dimensional space}}{\text{Aggregate labor expenses}}$$

Formularized writing of the criterion:

$$CCC = \frac{a_1 + b_1i + m_1j + a_2 + b_2i + C_2j}{(a_1 + b_1i) + (a_2 + b_2i)} = \frac{GDP_1 + GDP_2}{(a_1 + b_1i) + (a_2 + b_2i)}$$

where $(a_1 + b_1i)$—expenses connected to the creation of Internet values

$(a_2 + b_2i)$—expenses connected to the creation of Internet services

VARIETY OF CRITERIA REFLECTING THE MOVEMENT OF COMPLEX INTERNET PRODUCT

In the frames of the following criterion correlate GDP placed in the three-dimensional space, in proportion with past labor expenses.

$$AAA_1 = \frac{b_1i + m_1j + b_2i + C_2j}{a_1 + a_2} = \frac{NDP_1 + NDP_2}{a_1 + a_2}$$

In the frames of the next criterion we correlate aggregate NDP measuring with the direct labor expenses.

$$AAA_2 = \frac{b_1i + m_1j + b_2i + C_2j}{b_1i + b_2i} = \frac{NDP_1 + NDP_2}{b_1i + b_2i}$$

We proportionately correlate NI with past labor expenses.

$$AAA_3 = \frac{b_1i + m_1j + b_2i + C_2j}{(a_1 + b_1i) + (a_2 + b_2i)} = \frac{NDP_1 + NDP_2}{(a_1 + b_1i) + (a_2 + b_2i)}$$

Apart from the criteria in question there is another group of them:

In the frames of the following criterion we correlate in measure aggregate GDP with direct labor expenses.

$$BBB_1 = \frac{m_1j + C_2j}{a_1 + a_2} = \frac{NI}{a_1 + a_2}$$

In the variant below we compare economic product, NDP with past labor expenses.

$$BBB_2 = \frac{m_1j + C_2j}{b_1i + b_2i} = \frac{NI}{b_1i + b_2i}$$

$$BBB_3 = \frac{m_1j + C_2j}{(a_1 + b_1i) + (a_2 + b_2i)} = \frac{NI}{(a_1 + b_1i) + (a_2 + b_2i)}$$

4. GENERALIZED SYSTEM OF CRITERIA REFLECTING THE MOVEMENT OF COMPLEX INTERNET PRODUCT

$$CCC_1 = \frac{GDP}{\text{Aggregate labor expenses}} = \frac{a_1 + b_1i + m_1j + a_2 + b_2i + C_2j}{(a_1 + b_1i) + (a_2 + b_2i)}$$

$$CCC_2 = \frac{NDP}{\text{Aggregate labor expenses}} = \frac{b_1i + m_1j + b_2i + C_2j}{(a_1 + b_1i) + (a_2 + b_2i)}$$

$$CCC_3 = \frac{NDP}{\text{Aggregate labor expenses}} = \frac{m_1j + C_2j}{(a_1 + b_1i) + (a_2 + b_2i)}$$

OPERATIONS WITH COMPLEX NUMBERS

The application of complex numbers in the economic theory of Internet sphere enables us not only to revise traditional attitudes in assessing the results of functioning of its branches or evaluating the criteria of efficiency of resource utilization but also to introduce changes in technology of calculation of expenses, results and criteria.

With the commitment of complex numbers we transit over to the realm of unconventional arithmetic and algebra where the rules of addition, subtraction, multiplication and division have specific features. They vary from the operations we are accustomed to in daily life.

The addition of aggregated economic indices is performed according to the formula:

a) $z_1 + z_2 = (a_1 + b_1i) + (a_2 + b_2i) = (a_1 + a_2) + (b_1i + b_2i)$

b) $z_1 - z_2 = (a_1 + b_1i) - (a_2 + b_2i) = (a_1 - a_2) + (b_1i - b_2i)$

c) $z_1z_2 = (a_1 + b_1i) \times (a_2 + b_2i) = a_1a_2 + a_1b_2i + a_2b_1i + b_1b_2i^2 = a_1a_2 + a_1b_2i$
$+ a_2b_1i - b_1b_2 = (a_1a_2 - b_1b_2) + (a_1b_2 + a_2b_1)i$

d)
$$\frac{z_1}{z_2} = \frac{a_1a_2 + b_1b_2}{a_2^2 + b_2^2} + \frac{(a_2b_1 - a_1b_2)i}{a_2^2 + b_2^2}$$

For quaternions:

$R1 + R2 = (a1 + a2) + (b1 + b2)i + (C1 + C2)j.$

$R1 - R2 = (a1 - a2) + (b1 - b2)i + (C1 - C2)j.$

where
$R_1 = a_1 + b_1i + C_1j \quad R_2 = a_2 + b_2i + C_2j.$

0-595-26322-4